WISDOM
TO SERVE

SERVANT LEADERSHIP IN A VOLATILE WORLD

WISDOM TO SERVE: SERVANT LEADERSHIP
IN A VOLATILE WORLD

Original material Copyright 2021
by Accent on Words Press and Shari Scott
ISBN 978-1-7342605-3-3
Library of Congress Control Number: 2021905449

Printed in the United States of America
by Ingram Content Group.

Published by Accent on Words Press
Address all queries to
18543 Devonshire Street #327
Northridge, California 91324
accentonwords.com

First Printing

Cover image by Almeida on Pixabay.
Butterfly image by Rebecca Read on Pixabay.
Cover design and copy by Deborah A. Jackson.
Edited by Deborah A. Jackson

Published in the United States, Canada, Europe
the United Kingdom, Australia, and New Zealand.

WISDOM TO SERVE

SERVANT LEADERSHIP IN A VOLATILE WORLD

Dr. Shari D. Scott

Accent on Words Press

This book is dedicated to those organizations seeking to enhance their business from conception to sustainability. My prayer is that God will grace you to fulfill the work or vision to which He has called you.

ACKNOWLEDGEMENTS

I have been fortunate to know many people in my life who believe in me and have supported me throughout my life-journey. First, I wish to thank my mother for giving me the strength to pursue my dreams and the resilience to overcome life's challenges.

To my friends, Paula Johnson and Dr. Patrick D. Ross, who inspired me to pursue a doctoral degree, thank you for your love, patience, prayers, and support on countless study nights. Next to the Lord, you two have been my driving force and inspiration to achieve the completion of this portfolio.

To my family, who have been so supportive of my educational pursuits throughout the years, I love every one of you! I could not have made it without your constant prayers, love, and encouragement. To my church family, Greater New Light Baptist Church, whose unfailing faith, prayers, and belief in my ability to succeed have thrust me forward, thank you.

I would like to extend my gratitude to my doctoral chair, Dr. Nancy J. Duresky, for the support and guidance she showed me throughout my writing and for her remarkable level of rigor and commitment to academic excellence. To Dr. Tora Brown, I give thanks for her openness and willingness to share knowledge and support during the field placement. Professor Del Black, Dr. Robert, Clark, Dr. Leon Tonkonogy, and Dr. Kevin Walsh, I am indebted to you for your guidance, encouragement, and outstanding level of professionalism. Thank you for sharing your knowledge and learning experiences with me.

Finally, to my wonderful, smart, bright, intelligent, and amazing doctoral cohort, who made learning fun again: Alice Nkore, Brandi Reid, Bennett Annan, Kristyl Smith, Lisa-Mone Lamontagne, Margaret Easter, Melanie Gharapetian, Jamie Menendez-Adamski, Greg Hilsenrath, James Golden, Sherman Mitchell, Raffi Islikaplan, Ramila Sara Naziri, Debbie Jackson, *"You are smart, you are kind, and you are important!"* Thanks for making the journey so enjoyable and being the best cohort ever! #classof2019!

CONTENTS

INTRODUCTION

Many scholars have argued for the usefulness of understanding leadership styles and leadership theory (Brooks, 2009; Daft, 2011; De Pree, 2004; Glanz, 2002; Greenleaf, 1991; Kouzes & Posner, 1995; Leithwood & Riehl, 2003). An understanding of these leadership theories assists business process consultants in diagnosing issues and designing interventions useful to a given organization. Understanding a leader's personal style and helping that leader choose more effective interaction styles for a given context can also assist a consultant in designing effective interventions.

This book grew out a field placement engagement during the summer of 2018 as I was attaining my doctorate in organizational psychology. The field placement took place in a church organization that was planning to expand its community outreach programs. The experience I had at this organization was similar in some ways to my first field placement during my doctoral education. Additionally, it was similar to what I encountered in previous consulting engagements at religious-based institutions, where I experienced leadership in a way that was different from what might be found, for example, in a for-profit business. The organization for this case study was led by a generous-natured man with a deeply rooted desire to "do good." Yet this leader did not possess the strong business skills necessary to develop the church or its individual programs as a "business" from conception to sustainability.

Because I had observed this situation before, I had a personal vision based on assisting religious leaders who struggle with the business aspects of managing a church. My desire is to help organizational leaders become more effective by utilizing tools that will aid leaders in moving their organization forward. One outcome of publishing this book would be to help me achieve that goal.

In the first section of this book, the literature and theories relevant to consulting within organizations and coaching executives are reviewed. This includes scholarship that examines the relationship between servant leadership and nonprofit organizations. This is followed by a section on leadership theories, and another section devoted solely to servant leadership. After that, there are two case studies: one about The Walt Disney Company, and then a description of a consultation from my personal experience.

THE CONCEPT OF LEADERSHIP

There has been continuing interest among scholars in the concept of leadership (Brooks, 2009). Some scholars have defined leadership based on personal characteristics or virtues, such as courage, impartiality, empathy, judgement, enthusiasm, humility, and imagination (Glanz, 2002). De Pree (2004) and others defined leadership as more "tribal than scientific . . . more of a weaving of relationships than an amassing of information" (p. 9). Kouzes and Posner (1995) wrote that a leader encourages the heart of others, while Leithwood and Riehl (2003) stated that leadership is an influence process that can lead to positive results and outcomes. Among these scholars, a common thread is the idea that leadership is based on relationships, influence on others, and achieving positive results and outcomes.

The practice of effective leadership is often directional in that it is aimed at a given achievement. It can be used as a vehicle moving toward continuing and achieving purpose. For example, in organizations, leadership is usually meant to directly or indirectly influence stakeholders for the attainment of a common goal. Most often, the goal of leadership in considered a positive outcome. Burns (1978) stated, "All leadership is goal oriented. Successful leadership points in a direction and is the vehicle of continuing and achieving purpose" (p. 455).

In alignment with Burns (1978), Leithwood and Riehl (2003) emphasized that leadership provides purpose and direction. Leaders can provide purpose and direction to followers by articulating the organizational vision, embodying the organization's values, and creating an environment in which goals can be realized and achieved (Richards & Engle, 1986). This is accomplished during face-to-face interactions or through other communication events. De Pree (2004) stated that the signs of an effective leader can be found among the followers. Further, the first responsibility of the leader is to define the current environment—the last, to say thank you.

At best, an effective leader ensures that the accomplishments of the organization are shared among leaders and followers, with everyone fully engaged and accepting responsibility for the tasks and accomplishments. Johnson and Johnson (2013) confirmed this belief by qualifying a leader as "a person who can influence others to be more effective in working to achieve their mutual goals and maintain effective working relationships among members" (p. 58).

Leadership vs. Management

De Pree (2004) distinguished leadership from management. He argued that leadership deals with people and relationships. By contrast, the function of management involves data and products. Leaders tackle the ambiguity and the "messiness" of human relationships, that is, the complex inner lives of beings within their organization. In comparison, management primarily addresses numbers and inanimate objects. In organizations, supervisors and executives are encouraged to be more than managers. Since organizations are ever-evolving, leaders can be more effective by keeping their heads and hearts attuned to their followers, because "relationships count more than structure" (De Pree, 2004, p. 28).

Servant Leadership

A somewhat recent concept, the idea of the "servant leader" was first introduced by Greenleaf (1970). Greenleaf suggested that servant leadership "is the desire to serve one another, and to serve something beyond ourselves, a higher purpose" (p. 59). Greenleaf also stated that the catalyst for his thoughts about servant leadership was crystalized as he read Hesse's (1956) short novel, *Journey to the East.*

Greenleaf summarized his interpretation of the meaning of the novel by stating, "The great leader is seen as a servant first, and that simple fact is the key to his greatness" (p. 2). Greenleaf described different attributes of the servant leader, who "initiates, provides the ideas and the structure, and takes the risk of failure along with the chance of success" (p. 8).

The focus of the servant leader is on the followers of the organization or on those served by the organization (Stone, Russell, & Patterson, 2004). The servant leader is self-reflective and asks him or herself: Do those I serve grow as people? Do they, while being served, become healthier, wiser, freer, more autonomous, more likely themselves to become servants? What is the effect on the least privileged in society? Will they benefit, or, at least, will they not be further deprived? (Greenleaf, 1991).

When Greenleaf first proposed the theory of the servant leader, the concept was only descriptive and was not grounded in current thought on leadership. Several scholars have studied the construct and have incorporated it within current scholarship. Wong and Page (2003) argued that the development of a servant leader involved four orientations: character, people, task, and process.

Character is based on personal traits in that the servant leader serves others with humility and honesty. The people orientation addresses humanity, focusing on the emotions of the follower or members, teaching them how to get along with others and helping them explore their full potential. This orientation looks at how leaders handle their jobs, inclusive of the methods, the formula of the projects, and the establishment of a vision.

A servant leader's core value is love, and this core value is used as the basis to develop future behaviors. The servant leader's traits come from this belief in and practice of empathy. These leaders are willing to listen, try to satisfy the needs of others, and encourage and serve others. They also create vision and values, set up an environment for teamwork, and are ready to empower others to pursue the goals set for the organization.

Additionally, researchers have argued that there is a type

of leadership unique to religious organizations beyond servant leadership (Strebel, 1996).

Hernez-Broome and Boyce (2011) defined spiritual leadership as providing guidance in matters of faith in a higher power. Guidance is provided not only through what the leader says but also by the leader's behaviors. Additional styles of leadership, as defined by Daft (2011), include:

Achievement-Oriented Leadership: Achievement-oriented leaders show confidence in subordinates and assist them in learning how to achieve high goals. This type of leader sets clear and challenging goals for subordinates as well as for himself/herself. That is, this leader's behavior stresses high-quality performance and improvement over current performance (Johnson & Johnson, 2013).

Autocratic Leadership: Autocratic leadership represents a more extreme version of transactional leadership, as autocratic leaders have significant control over staff and rarely consider worker suggestions or share power. This type of leader is known to rule with an iron fist and is rarely appreciated by staff, which can lead to high turnover and absenteeism. There can also be a lack of creativity due to strategic direction coming from a single individual. This leadership style is best suited to environments where jobs are routine or require limited skills. It is also common in military organizations (Strebel, 1996).

Bureaucratic Leadership: Bureaucratic leadership models are most often implemented in highly regulated or administrative environments, where adherence to the rules and a defined hierarchy are important.

One can see this structure in churches, as those who serve in administrative roles often ensure that people follow the rules and carry out tasks by the book. While this style of leadership works well in certain roles—such as health and safety—it can stifle innovation and creativity in more agile, fast-paced companies (Luecke, 2003).

Charismatic Leadership: There is a certain amount of overlap between charismatic and transformational leadership. Both styles rely heavily on the positive charm and personality of the leader in question. However, charismatic leadership is usually considered less favorable, largely because the success of projects and initiatives is closely linked to the presence of the leader. While transformational leaders build confidence in a team that remains when they move on, the removal of a charismatic leader typically leaves a power vacuum (Luecke, 2003).

Democratic Leadership: Democratic leadership is also known as participative leadership; this style means leaders often ask for input from team members before making a final decision.

Workers usually report higher levels of job satisfaction in these environments, and the company can benefit from better creativity. On the downside, the democratic process is normally slower and may not function well in workplaces in which quick decision making is crucial (Daft, 2011).

Directive Leadership: Directive leaders tell subordinates exactly what they are supposed to do. Leader behavior includes planning, making schedules, setting performance goals and behavior standards, and stressing adherence to rules and regulations. Directive leadership behavior is similar to the initiating structure or task-oriented leadership (Poulfelt & Olson, 2009).

Laissez-faire Leadership: This type of leadership is commonly used to describe economic environments. In French, *laissez-faire* literally means "let them do," though it is typically translated "let it be." As such, laissez-faire leaders are characterized by their hands-off approach, allowing employees to get on with tasks as they see fit.

This can be effective in creative jobs or workplaces where employees are very experienced. However, it is important that these leaders monitor performance and effectively communicate expectations to prevent work standards from slipping (Daft, 2011).

Situational Leadership: Situational leadership is based on a theory that effective leaders utilize a range of different styles depending on the circumstances or environment. Factors such as worker seniority, the business process being performed, and the complexity of relevant tasks all play an important role in what leadership style to adopt for any given situation.

However, many people have an embedded leadership style, which can make switching between roles challenging. It can also be difficult to gauge what style is most suitable for certain circumstances. This can result in delaying forward progress, including decision-making processes (Poulfelt & Olson, 2009).

Transactional Leadership: The basis of transactional leadership is a transaction or exchange process between leaders and followers. The transactional leader recognizes followers' needs and desires and then clarifies how those needs and desires will be satisfied in exchange for meeting specified objectives or performing certain duties. Thus, followers receive rewards for job performance, whereas leaders benefit from the completion of tasks (Poulfelt & Olson, 2009).

Transformational Leadership: This leadership style is

characterized by the ability to bring about significant change in both the company's followers and in the organization. Transformational leaders can bring about changes in an organization's vision, strategy, and culture as well as promote innovation in products, services, and technologies. The transformational leadership style is based on the personal values, beliefs, and qualities of the leader rather than on an exchange process between leaders and followers (Daft, 2011).

Leadership Means Relationship

In sum, many traits and abilities have been associated with various styles of successful leaders, yet Kotter (1995) argued that traits alone are not sufficient to guarantee effective leadership. Furthermore, implied among the various styles of leadership are different types of relationships. As such, the concept of leadership can be defined in terms of relationships with others or influence on followers in order to achieve a shared purpose.

The Importance of Organizational Leadership

Leadership is a critical element and an influential aspect of all businesses. Leaders possess the skills and tools that influence and inspire followers, consequently allowing for competence and the efficient operation of the organization. Effective leaders understand the vision, mission, objectives, and action plans of the organization that they serve so that they can lead their workforce into realizing the company's goals. Beyond a shadow of a doubt, a good leader plays a significant role in achieving success for the enterprise.

Organizational leadership is vital, because leaders motivate, influence, energize, and communicate with their team members to bring out the best in them to promote the advancement of the organization. Leaders are catalysts for success, and they always challenge and encourage their staff to think and act differently for the best interest of the team and company (Showry & Manasa, 2014). It is of interest that challenging the status quo is a fundamental dilemma that can lead to success.

Leaders are also goal-setters; they determine the direction a team will take and position the company in a way that it will advance. Furthermore, a revolutionary leader transforms a business, group, or department. While facing the realities of business, these leaders are able to mobilize primary resources to achieve the objectives and goals of the organization. When challenges inevitably arise, leaders think through the problems and discover a path through them, appropriately directing the team and activating the tools necessary to continue efficient processes (Priest & Gass, 2017).

Effective leaders have sharp intellects and a variety of experiences in the field of leadership enabling them to make quick judgment calls that affect the state of the organization. They are often risk-takers who have an eye for assessing good and bad risks, thus making calculated moves to mitigate threats to the enterprise. Good leadership ensures that the company fully utilizes its ability to conduct business at maximum capacity.

Nedelea and Gupta (2015) confirmed this perspective of a leader. At one time, I concluded that a leader is someone who sits in an office and gives instructions, because that is what I experienced. Yet these scholars underscored that good leaders participate in some of the duties and responsibilities of the team, including those that they have authority to delegate. Familiarity with the most basic and advanced functions of a unit or department allows leaders to be more effective in their role as opposed to those who only have a theoretical framework.

Organizations need leaders of excellent quality; such leaders will seek out the best performers in every aspect of the enterprise. It is also noteworthy that leaders empower and encourage team members to do their best for the sake of enhancing the company (Nedelea & Gupta, 2015).

Showry and Manasa (2014) illustrated that excellent managerial proficiencies come about when personal skills, such as self-awareness, are exhibited in a leader. Effective management requires more than just a degree or to be in a particular age group; one must possess adequate interpersonal skills, which contribute to self-actualization. Further, Showry and Manasa (2014) identified self-awareness as the primary requirement for every effective leader. Self-awareness enables leaders to understand the tasks at hand, what they are to achieve, and how they will go about it.

Yet it is not valid to see leaders and managers only as individuals who carry the ultimate power or to perceive them as having little to no flaws. However, self-aware leaders embrace their imperfections and relentlessly seek to become better by leveraging their weaknesses and failures (Akins, Bright, Brunson, & Wortham, 2013). Without the acknowledgment of a leader's strengths and weaknesses, there is a high likelihood that a unit, department, or team will not attain success.

After studying organizational leadership, my understanding and perspectives have been significantly enhanced. One of the areas that has been illuminated for me is the idea of self-realization. Leadership is not just about leading a team of people; it is also about leading oneself toward further growth and development. An individual who does not have the internal initiative for personal development is not fit to direct an organization toward growth.

As a leader, I also want to become more self-aware and gain additional insight into my strengths and weaknesses for the sake of being more efficient in achieving goals and in handling managerial matters as effectively as is possible (Aktas, Gelfand, & Hanges, 2016). Furthermore, effective decision making is one of the most critical aspects of leadership. Obtaining useful insights can only enhance an individual's leadership qualities with the aim of success for team members, organizations, and their stakeholders.

Leadership in the Nonprofit Sector

Nonprofit organizations (NPOs) have served a pivotal and continually growing role in the United States (Anheier, 2014). The term "nonprofit" refers to an organization that operates for the common good and not for generating individual wealth. Nonprofit organizations do not distribute their profits to individuals who control the organization, such as clients, officers, a board of directors, stockholders, owners, volunteers, employees, or trustees (irs.gov, n.d.a). While a nonprofit organization can make a profit, the profit it earns must be used toward the core mission of the organization and not toward any personal benefit (Boyes & Melvin, 2011).

The Internal Revenue Service (IRS) has classified more than 20 categories of NPOs, which can be divided into two main types: 501(c)(3) and 501(c)(4), according to the criteria of tax-exempt organizations (irs.gov, n.d.b). Although there are similarities between these two types of nonprofits, since both are classified by the IRS as tax-exempt, there are also some distinctions.

First, 501(c)(3)s are strictly dedicated to benefit individuals within society and include religious, educational, or charitable organizations; they do not participate in politics or influence electoral processes, and individual contributions are tax deductible (Anheier, 2014). By contrast, 501(c)(4)s are dedicated to benefiting the public as a whole and include civic leagues, advocacy groups, organizations that lobby for the support of social and political issues; individual contributions to 501(c)(4)s are not tax deductible (Anheier, 2014).

NPOs provide a broad range of goods and services depending on type, purpose, and size of the organization (Worth, 2014). For example, among 501(c)(3)s are organizations such as the Ford Foundation and the Rockefeller Foundation, health NPOs, such as the Johns Hopkins Medical Corporation, and churches. Other NPOs provide human services, such as the YMCA and Meals on Wheels, and include universities, such as Harvard, Yale, and Stanford and many other organizations (Anheier, 2014). Examples of 501(c)(4)s include the American Action Network Inc., the Girls Scouts, and Californians Working Together to Restore Public Schools (Guidestar, n.d.).

A nonprofit charitable organization is governed by a

board of directors. Boards must make sure that the charitable nonprofit abides by the law and exercises financial responsibility. Board members can be held liable if they do not fulfill their fiduciary responsibilities. The overarching purpose of the board is to oversee the functions of the organization and the CEO so that the CEO can take actions to keep the activities of the organization in line with the mission of the organization and relevant laws. The purpose of the board of directors is oversight, not to direct or interfere with managing the day-to-day activities of the organization. An important guiding principle for members of an NPO's board of directors is that the organization's mission should be directed to the public good. Taken together, all of the guiding principles lead to planning and oversight of the organization on behalf of the public (International Federation of Accountants, 2014).

There are public disclosure requirements to inform all stakeholders about the organization and its major activities. Each year, nonprofits must report their activities to the IRS, including the salaries of key staff and the names of all donors who give more than $5,000 (International Federation of Accountants, 2014). Many donors use Form 990 (a public document) to find out how much of their contributions go to the nonprofit's programs and how much is used for fundraising efforts and administrative expenditures. While Form 990 for many years was primary viewed as a financial report, of late it has become a corporate governance best practices report that includes questions regarding whistleblower policies and allocation of contributions and expenses of programs (International Federation of Accountants, 2014).

The IRS is the major governing body for nonprofit organizations. One of the first tasks involved in forming a nonprofit organization is applying for tax-exempt, or 501(c)(3), status from the IRS. Part of this application includes writing bylaws to be approved by the organization's board of directors. Bylaws contain the organization's internal affairs guidebook. In the bylaws, procedures are established for holding elections, organizing meetings, quorum requirements, membership structure (if needed), and other essential operations of a nonprofit.

Organizational bylaws can function as an organizational manual and will help its leaders guide an organization's orderly operations. Unlike articles of incorporation, the IRS does not require any specific language to be included in nonprofit bylaws; however, they usually include references to the organization's structure and purpose as a reminder of the makeup of the nonprofit (Nonprofitally, n.d.).

Leadership in the Economic Sector

The nonprofit sector consists of voluntary, nonprofit organizations and associations (Anheier, 2014). For-profit organizations encompass the body of institutions whose primary goal is to make a profit (Boyes & Melvin, 2011). The public sector refers to the government and the agencies of government (Anheier, 2014).

One difference between a "nonprofit" and a "for-profit" organization is that a nonprofit cannot issue stocks, while a for-profit organization can issue stocks/equity shares for ownership. Stocks represent partial ownership of an institution. Nonprofits have no direct ownership—they exist for the benefit of society. If a nonprofit is dissolved or liquidated, it can only transfer its assets to another nonprofit organization. It cannot distribute the assets among its employees or members of the board of directors. If a for-profit organization is liquidated, the assets can be apportioned and distributed amongst its constituent members. Additionally, a nonprofit organization can seek a tax exemption, while a for-profit organization is generally not exempted from paying taxes.

Competition from privatization has forced many NPOs to act more like their for-profit competitors (Anheier, 2014) by adopting business concepts, such as strategic planning, financial benchmarks, budgeting, and marketing. There have been advantages and disadvantages associated with this change. An advantage of NPOs adopting business practices has been the implementation of generally accepted accounting principles (GAAP) used in NPO financial statements. Some nonprofits have adopted Sarbanes-Oxley financial standards to professionalize their internal accounting processes (Worth, 2014). Further, some NPOs have developed business strategic plans to strengthen their marketing. Another advantage of NPOs adopting for-profit business standards is that NPOs have leveraged these strategies by designing and selling a variety of products, including license plate holders, items in museum stores, and products with their logos in order to generate revenue.

There are potential disadvantages when NPOs adopt typical for-profit business operations and standards. Anheier (2014) argued that some NPOs fear becoming so financially driven that they lose their focus on helping the clients they serve. Anheier (2014) contended further that this concern, in part, is due to the gap between theories of economics, supply and demand, and frameworks for capturing social value. Social value is a broad concept and outside of the scope of this portfolio; yet nonprofit consultants can help NPOs remain competitive by recognizing the strengths and opportunities of social enterprise and develop interventions that bridge the gap between traditional goods and services versus providing social value.

Organizational Structure Design Theory

Barksdale and Lund (2006) encouraged all for-profit and nonprofit organizations to develop a mission statement that delineates the purpose of the organization. Executive managers along with the board of directors decide the organization's strategic intent, including a specific mission to be accomplished (Daft, 2011). The mission statement, or organizational goal(s), states the organization's reason for existence and describes the organization's shared values and beliefs. The board and chief executive, therefore, design the structure of an organization.

Bagley and Dauchy (2013) argued that there are two concepts of organizational structure design: structural dimensions and contingency factors. Structural dimensions are internal aspects of the organization that focus on infrastructure, including centralized management versus decentralized management, specialized tasks or empowered roles, formal or informal processes, vertical or horizontal communication, and hierarchy of authority or collaborative teamwork (Bagley & Dauchy, 2013).

Contingency factors are different from structural design in that contingency factors are focused on both internal and external factors that address organizational type, including organizational size (large or small), business strategy (efficiency or innovation), organizational environment (stable or changing), organizational culture (rigid or adaptive), and technology used (culture and manufacturing) (Waclawski & Church, 2002). Depending on the choices in each aspect of the structural dimensions and contingency factors, an organization can be classified as having a mechanistic or organic structural design. When an organization is classified as having a mechanistic design, management decisions are usually made at the top of the hierarchy. Conversely, when an organization is classified as having an organic structure, decisions are made corporately throughout the entire structure of the organization.

Organizational Design Models

The Mechanistic Model	The Organic Model
Emphasizes importance of achieving high levels of production and efficiency through:	Emphasizes importance of achieving high levels of production and efficiency through:
• Extensive use of rules and procedures • Centralized authority • High specialization of labor	• Limited use of rules and procedures • Decentralized authority • Relatively low degrees of specialization

The mechanistic design is a traditional organizational model influenced by Max Weber and Frederick Taylor (Shafritz & Hyde, 2011). In these organizations, tasks are specified by function. The organization is ruled/governed, and the chain of command is followed. Additionally, it has been argued that Frederick Taylor wanted to control the shop floor workers to create efficiency (Shafritz & Hyde, 2011). A mechanistic design was the foundation for many organizational theories that continue to be in practice, although the model is seen as outdated in many industries (Shafritz & Hyde, 2011).

There are advantages and disadvantages of a mechanistic design. The benefits of having a mechanical model of organizations include predictability, given the high structure of procedures. Some believe it is an advantage for decisions to be made at the top of the hierarchy, so there is little room for deviation and efficiency in production (Greenwood & Miller, 2006).

The disadvantages of having a mechanistic organizational structure model are behavioral rigidity. Additional difficulty in adhering to strict procedures can be problematic as well as resistance to change and oppressive behavioral control of employees. Additionally, a mechanistic structure can impede organizational learning (Brooks, 2009). Another disadvantage of the mechanistic model is that it tends to limit creativity and flexibility.

In contrast to the top-down decision making of the mechanistic model, organic structural design means that decisions come mainly from non-executive levels and flow to the executive level. Roles in organic structural models are dynamic and allow for innovation. There are few rules; communication originates from all directions.

In organic organizational structural models, teamwork is encouraged. The advantages of having an organic design are flexibility for change. Additionally, all members and employees are expected and encouraged to contribute, including playing a part in organizational learning (Greenwood & Miller, 2006).

The possible disadvantages of having an organic structural design include having too much information coming from all areas. Additionally, consensus is needed from all team members for change. This can retard change and take more time than in a mechanistic model (Greenwood & Miller, 2006).

Organizations may be tempted to choose the organizational structure model they believe is "good" or "better." However, "no approach is suitable for every organization, but each offers some advantages that the others may lack" (Picardi & Masick, 2013).

Consultant Interface with Organizations

Block (2011) suggested that consultants learn how to exhibit two qualities in the following order: 1) The first quality is technical skills, which encompasses the ability to understand a client's concern; once understood, the consultant can offer expertise. 2) The next quality is interpersonal skills. Interpersonal skills include self-confidence, patience, and endurance. According to Block, with these three qualities under one's belt, there is a high probability for success. These qualities are important, as "competition for management consultants is likely to remain keen, and those with the most education and experience will have the best prospects" (Bradberry & Greaves, 2009).

Organizational Lifecycle

Organizational structure design theory provides a partial roadmap for understanding and explaining the way people in organizations behave, make decisions, communicate, and develop strategy. It also provides insight into the influence of the structure and the effectiveness primarily of how the processes in place affect employee performance. There are four major stages of organizational development (Greiner, 1992): the entrepreneurial stage, collectivity stage, formalization stage, and elaboration stage.

Entrepreneurship Stage: The first stage is known as the entrepreneurial stage, and the name fits quite well. At this point, the organization is small, there is little hierarchy, and employees work in many different parts of the organization. Supervision is limited in focus, and effort is primarily placed on the product and/or service the organization provides. This stage of the lifecycle is easy to see when looking at new start-ups.

One issue in the entrepreneurial stage is the lack of leadership. Although this usually does not cause any issues early on, it can become an issue as the organization starts to expand. When the number of employees hits a certain point (i.e., 30 to 40), leadership is required to keep the different parts of an organization intact.

Crisis Element in Stage One. As the organization starts to grow, having a larger number of employees can give rise to problems. Creative and technically oriented company owners are confronted with management issues, but they may prefer to focus their energies on making and selling the product or inventing new products and services. At this time of crisis, entrepreneurs must either adjust the structure of the organization to accommodate continued growth or else bring in strong managers who can do so (Daft, 2011).

By way of example, when Apple began a period of rapid

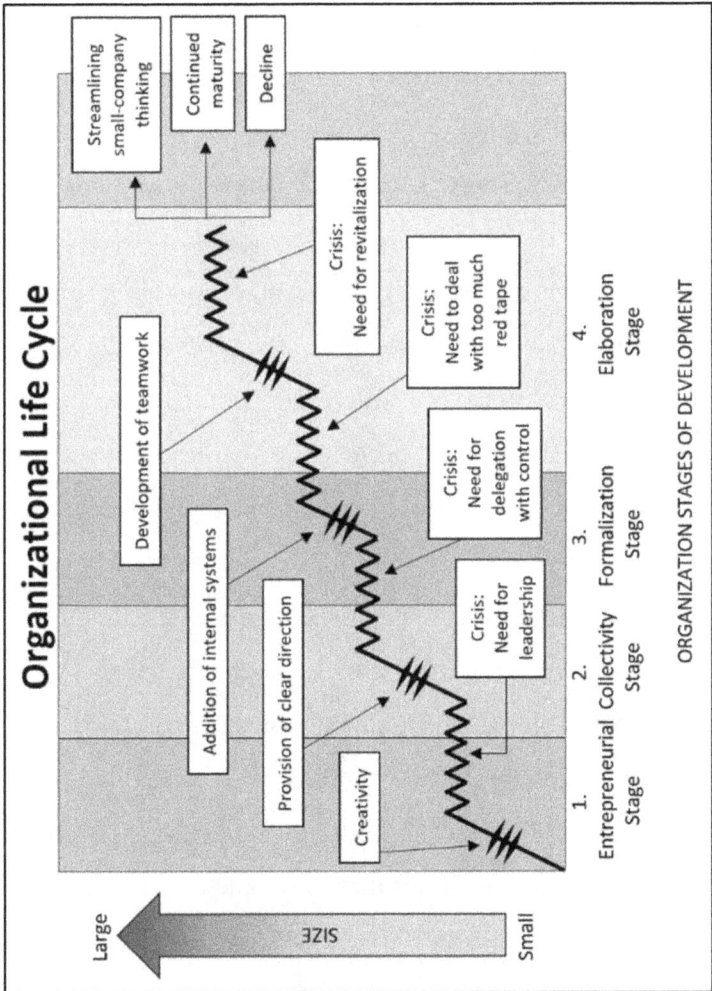

Organizational Life Cycle

Streamlining small-company thinking

Continued maturity

Decline

Crisis: Need for revitalization

Development of teamwork

Crisis: Need to deal with too much red tape

Addition of internal systems

Crisis: Need for delegation with control

Provision of clear direction

Crisis: Need for leadership

Creativity

SIZE

Large

Small

1. Entrepreneurial Stage

2. Collectivity Stage

3. Formalization Stage

4. Elaboration Stage

ORGANIZATION STAGES OF DEVELOPMENT

growth, A.C. Markkula was brought in as a leader because neither Jobs nor Wozniak was qualified or cared to manage the expanding company (Gustin, 2010).

Collectivity Stage: Once leadership is established and the employee base has increased, the organization goes into what is known as the collectivity stage. At this point the organization has begun to develop clear goals and direction. Creativity and flexibility still exist, but now there are boundaries that were not evident in the entrepreneurship stage. In large organizations divisions begin to emerge, and employees start to focus on more related and specific tasks. Communication is still open and informal.

Crisis Element in the Collectivity Stage. The collectivity stage is characterized by the growth of the organization in that it is too big for one or two upper managers to direct or control. It becomes extremely difficult for a single person or small number of people to manage multiple groups closely and effectively. What may occur is that lower-level managers emerge from the groups and are named as leaders of individual teams. This allows upper management to communicate indirectly with all the different parts of the organization without talking to each employee individually.

Formalization Stage: This is the stage in which an organization transitions from an informal environment to a more formal, regulated environment. Multiple layers of management are created, causing communication to become formal. Employees are generally constrained to their section of the organization, and lower/middle management handles communication between groups.

Crisis Element in the Formalization Stage. One main issue in this stage is the growing amount of red tape. Some scholars have indicated that bureaucracy develops after such regulation becomes detrimental to the organization.

Middle managers become buried within the organization and have little input into decisions in upper management or lower development. Due to the multiple layers of management, innovation becomes difficult to bring to the surface, develop, and implement. Requests must now travel through layers of representatives and regulations before they arrive at the intended destination.

Elaboration stage. In this final stage, the organization works toward sustainability. At this point, the organization is forced to change its structure, or the lack of innovation and communication will eventually destroy the business. Management is forced to flatten, that is, reduce layers. Additionally, top management gives development groups more decision-making freedom. In many cases, traditional managers either must change their management style or leave the organization.

Crisis Element in the Elaboration Stage. During this stage the organization experiences a need for revitalization. After the organization reaches maturity, it may enter periods of temporary decline. As a result, a need for organizational change may occur. This usually happens every ten to twenty years. It can occur as a result of the organization shifting out of alignment with its environment.

Another cause may be that the organization becomes slow moving and over-bureaucratized. This is a stage of streamlining and innovation. Top managers are often replaced during this period (Lumen Learning, n.d.).

Organizational Characteristics During the Lifecycle

Starting and growing a business is a challenge (Brooks, 2009). Each time an organization enters a new stage in the lifecycle, it enters a new set of rules and norms for how the organization functions internally and how it relates to the external environment (Shelton, 2014). In fact, 84% of businesses that make it past the first year still fail within five years because they cannot make the transition out of the entrepreneurial stage (Shelton, 2014).

These transitions become even more difficult as organization progresses through additional stages of the lifecycle. As an organization evolves through the four stages of the lifecycle, changes take place in structure, control systems, innovation, and goals (Shelton, 2014).

While change does not happen easily, good leaders can help their organization adapt to external threats and new opportunities (Kotter, 1995). When leading a major change project, it is useful for leaders to recognize that the organization goes through change. Leaders are responsible for guiding employees and the organization through the change process (Daft, 2011).

Group Development

Groups are commonly used to accomplish tasks in today's business environments (Lencioni, 1998). Scholars have studied how groups develop over time (Johnson & Johnson, 2013), and perhaps the best-known scheme for group development was advanced by Tuckman (1965). Initially, Tuckman identified four stages of group development, which included forming, storming, norming, and performing. He believed that these stages are universal to all teams without regard to the group's members, purpose, goal, culture, location, or demographics.

Group Development

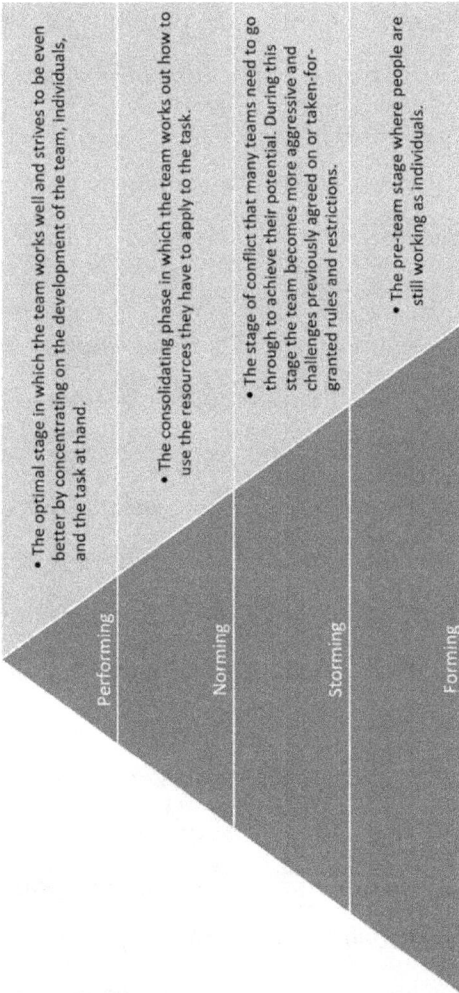

Performing
- The optimal stage in which the team works well and strives to be even better by concentrating on the development of the team, individuals, and the task at hand.

Norming
- The consolidating phase in which the team works out how to use the resources they have to apply to the task.

Storming
- The stage of conflict that many teams need to go through to achieve their potential. During this stage the team becomes more aggressive and challenges previously agreed on or taken-for-granted rules and restrictions.

Forming
- The pre-team stage where people are still working as individuals.

Forming Stage: The first stage of group development is known as the forming stage. The forming stage represents a time when the group is just starting to come together and is characterized by anxiety and uncertainty. Members are cautious with their behavior, which is driven by the desire to be accepted by all members of the group.

Members of the group avoid conflict, controversy, and personal opinions, even though they are beginning to form impressions of each other and gain an understanding of what the group will do together. Some believe this cautious behavior prevents the group from getting any real work done. However, the focus for group members during the forming stage is on becoming familiar with each other and their purpose, not on work.

Typical outcomes of the forming stage include gaining an understanding of the group's purpose, determining how the team will be organized and who will be responsible for what, discussion of major milestones or phases needed to reach the group's goal (including a rough project schedule), outlining general group rules (including when they will meet), and discovery of what resources will be available for the group to use.

Storming Stage: Individuals in the group can only be extremely polite until it is necessary to disagree. Important issues start to be addressed. Some people's patience will break early, and minor confrontations will arise that are addressed quickly or glossed over. These may relate to the work of the group itself or to roles and responsibilities within the group. Some will observe that it is good to be getting into the real issues, while others will wish to remain in the comfort and security of the forming stage.

Depending on the culture of the organization and individuals, conflicts will be more or less suppressed, but they will be there, under the surface. To deal with the conflict, individuals may feel they are winning or losing battles and will look for structural clarity and rules to prevent conflicts from persisting.

Norming Stage: This is the phase in which the group

really starts to function and work together as a team. Having had their arguments, they now understand each other better and can appreciate one another's skills and experience. Individuals start to understand the others' work habits and ethics, and everything seems much more natural.

Responsibilities and roles are much more clearly defined, expectations are set, and collaboration is in full swing. Individuals listen to each other, appreciate and support each other, and are prepared to change preconceived views; they now feel they are part of a cohesive, effective group.

Performing Stage: According to Tuckman (1965), not all teams will reach this phase, but those who have grown and become both knowledgeable and efficient at what they do, may attain it. Supervision goes down as individuals are now capable of making appropriate decisions. This is essentially when the team starts to shine and deliver superior results (Johnson & Johnson, 2013).

Ten years after first describing the four stages, Tuckman (1965) revisited his original work and described another stage: Adjourning. This stage is about completion and disengagement, both from the tasks and the group members. Adjourning gives individuals an opportunity to be proud of having achieved much and glad to have been part of such an enjoyable group.

Some authors describe Stage Five as "Deforming and Mourning," recognizing the sense of loss felt by group members (Chimaera Consulting Limited, 2001).

Tuckman's original work described the way he had observed groups evolve, whether they were conscious of it or not. Groups are often forming and changing, and each time that happens, they can move to a different Tuckman stage. A group might be happily norming or performing, but a new member might force them back into storming.

Seasoned leaders will be ready for this and will help the group get back to performing as quickly as possible. However, it is possible that some groups are fearful of moving back into storming or forward into performing. This fear will govern their behavior toward each other, especially their reaction to change (Chimaera Consulting Limited, 2001).

The Six Bases of Power

Although many scholars have examined the use of power in leadership, one of the first to study power, John R. P. French and Bertram Raven, developed a useful model. In 1959, these two social psychologists, through a study they conducted on power in leadership roles, identified five bases of power: coercive, reward, legitimate, referent, and expert (Johnson & Johnson, 2013).

In 1965, Raven revised this model to include a sixth form by separating the informational power base as distinct from the expert power base. The study demonstrated how different types of power affect leadership ability and success in a leadership role (Johnson & Johnson, 2013).

Reward Power: This is the power of a manager to give some type of reward to an employee in order to influence the employee to act. Rewards can be tangible or intangible.

The key distinction between tangible and intangible rewards is that tangible rewards are physical things and intangible rewards are not.

Examples of tangible rewards include monetary awards, wage or salary increases, bonuses, plaques, certificates, and gifts. Examples of intangible rewards include praise, positive feedback, recognition, more responsibility, including a rise in status, and even a well-timed "thank you."

Coercive Power: This is the ability of a manager to force an employee to follow an order by threatening the employee with punishment if the employee does not comply with the order. This form of power seeks to force or compel behavior rather than to influence behavior through persuasion.

Examples of coercive power include threats of write-ups, demotions, pay cuts, layoffs, and terminations if employees do not follow orders. To be effective, the manager must be able to follow through on the threat. While coercive power may be effective in the short-term, it can create serious problems for organizational effectiveness in the long run, as it tends to lower job satisfaction.

Constant turnover is costly, and it also hurts productivity, efficiency, and effectiveness. Additionally, some theorists argue that coercive leadership also stymies creativity and innovation, because employees are not much interested in taking risks and being creative if they live in an environment of fear and insecurity.

Legitimate Power: The power that leaders get by default due to their position in an organization is known as legitimate power. Leaders are essentially distinguished from followers due to the greater rights and responsibilities they have. That is, the additional rights that legitimate power bestows on them distinguishes leaders from followers. In a large organization, there is a power structure, and every leader has some higher authority to answer to, unless that leader is at the very apex of the power pyramid.

Referent Power: This is the power of an individual over the team (or followers), based on a high level of identification with, admiration of, or respect for the powerholder/leader. Nationalism, patriotism, celebrities, mass leaders, and widely respected people are examples of referent power in effect as defined by Bertram Raven and his colleagues.

Expert Power: Expert power is based upon employee perception that a manager or some other member of an organization has a high level of knowledge or a specialized set of skills that other employees or members of the organization do not possess. Expert power can actually turn power dynamics upside down, because its use is not limited to the formal leaders of an organization. Any member of an organization who has a high level of knowledge or a set of specialized skills that others in the organization do not possess may exert expert power.

Informational Power: Informational power occurs when a person possesses needed or wanted information. This is a short-term power that does not necessarily influence or build credibility. For example, a project manager may have all the information for a specific project, and that will give her "informational power" (Johnson & Johnson, 2013).

The Importance of Great Leadership

Leaders can shape people's lives. Johnson and Johnson (2013) defined a leader as a person who can influence others to be more effective in working to achieve their mutual goals and maintain effective working relationships among members. Leadership is the process through which leaders can exert such influence.

There are many different types of leadership styles.

Charismatic leaders have an emotional impact on people. They create an atmosphere of change, articulate an idealized vision of the future, inspire faith and hope, and frequently incur personal risks to influence followers (Daft, 2011).

Spiritual leadership, on the other hand, is the display of values, attitudes, and behaviors necessary to intrinsically motivate oneself and others toward a sense of spiritual expression through calling and memberships. Spiritual leadership also engages hope and faith to help the organization achieve desired outcomes. A leader's hope includes perseverance, endurance, goals and a clear expectation of victory through effort (Daft, 2011).

The effects of leadership can be difficult to identify, because successful goal achievement is the result of the coordinated efforts of many and is influenced by the actions of competitors, the discovery of new technologies, broad economic conditions, currency fluctuations, and many other factors beyond the control of leaders or their followers (Johnson & Johnson, 2013).

However, it is the belief of the consultant that the most valuable component of a leader is not power, position, influence, fame, talent, gifting, dynamic oratory, persuasiveness, intellectual superiority, academic achievement, or management skills—but character.

Character is the cradle of credibility for the leader.

Without the element of a strong, noble, and honorable character, all of a leader's potential achievements are in danger of being canceled by negative characteristics. Leaders are only as safe and secure as their character. Therefore, character is the most powerful force a leader can cultivate, because it protects leadership.

Having a strong character will enable leaders to be successful, personally and professionally, as they carry out their purpose, vision, and goals in life. Character is a force that can protect a leader's life, leadership, and legacy, because it manifests who the leader is and shapes who the leader will become. Without character, every other aspect of leadership is at risk.

MODERN LEADERSHIP THEORIES

Leadership is among the most multifaceted and complex phenomena to which organizational and psychological research are applied. The term "leader" has existed since the early 1300s and has been held in common vernacular since that time. A scientific study of leadership began in the twentieth century, and the majority of scholars who delved into the topic attempted to give explanations for it, providing particular thought to definitions.

Since leadership is still being studied and new leadership frameworks, methodologies, and styles are still taking shape today, it can be argued that leadership is one of the most observed but least understood phenomena of our time (Allen et al., 2016). Clearly, that is why there are numerous descriptions of leadership and why the research continues.

It is therefore important to review historical leadership theories and capture how they have evolved, how new methods developed, and to provide critical analysis of how modern leadership theories are being applied today.

The Evolution of Leadership Theory

Leadership is a subject that is widely taught in schools, colleges, universities, and businesses from its most basic form to the most prestigious. Various kinds of leadership in history are remembered for the mark they left in the world.

For instance, the Phoenicians introduced advanced glass-making techniques, navigational techniques, and phonetic alphabets. The Romans and Greeks are known for the autonomous styles of administration and analyses as well as their arts, construction, and calendars (Avey, Wernsing, & Palanski, 2012). Most of these societies were able to accomplish much because of the organized leadership styles and vision they executed.

Part of this continuing evolution of leadership, especially over the past century, has been from a practice to a process that includes research with the presentation of many leadership styles and theories.

The Great Man Theory

The Great Man Theory was motivated more by personal perspectives and opinions than by research. In 1840, Thomas Carlyle came up with the perception that leaders are born rather than "prepared" or "made." In the twentieth century, this notion developed into a philosophy and set of principles.

The Great Man Theory hypothesizes that front-runners or leaders are born and not prepared, taught, or developed. Carlyle assumed that the individual traits, inherent abilities, and prearranged (inherited) features produced the heroes who rose to rule the world. The supposition of the Great Man Theory, in essence, was that only a few persons possessed the obligatory characteristics and qualities that would authorize them to become active managers (Hoch et al., 2018). Reinforcing this idea, in 1869 Galton's research concluded that some leadership characteristics are delivered only from one group or linage to another via genetics.

Trait Theory

Trait Theory was an extension of the Great Man Theory that strove to prove scientifically that the world needed leaders with specific characteristics and that only a few people possessed such qualities.

Trait theory suggested that people were born with distinguishing features and dispositions, which together constituted a person's aptitude for leadership. It did, however, acknowledge that leaders could either be born or made and that people could learn the traits necessary to becoming a good leader. Some of these traits were documented by Stogdill in 1948, a study that was later expanded on by Mann in 1959. Stogdill released another study in 1974 and added more characteristics that illustrated the most powerful traits of a human leader (Joseph et al., 2015).

Behavioral Theory

Behavior theorists examined leaders' actions instead of their personality traits. The first view of behavior theory is that while leaders are attentive to completing an assignment or task, they are more concerned about group cohesiveness and individuality (Landis, Hill, & Harvey, 2014).

This view later developed into the Theory X and Y of leadership. Theory X proposed that most people detest their work; consequently, they desire to be well organized, since they cannot be efficient or perform well without order. Theory Y purported that individuals like their work; they are self-motivated and do not need coercion to behave responsibly (Landis, Hill, & Harvey, 2014).

Contingency and Situational Theories

Established in 1967 by Fiedler, contingency theory illustrated that explicit situations would determine the kind management responses required to address organizational situations effectively. It further recommended that leaders use various management approaches and methods.

Contingency theory is one of the most broadly researched of the leadership theories (Schedlitzki & Edwards, 2017).

Then in the 1960s, Blanchard developed situational leadership theory, which was built on a notion that unique circumstances needed varying rejoinders. This theory recommended that leaders adapt their governance to the developmental level of their followers. Leaders are expected to match their decision-making styles with the maturity level of employees (Allen et al., 2016).

These theories were practiced in the early to mid-twentieth century; further developments occurred more rapidly toward the end of that period and into the early twenty-first century. This earlier span of time was sometimes referred to as the anti-leadership era, because no theories about leadership styles in existence seemed universally agreeable.

This led to the ambiguity of the 1980s when some

theorists believed that leaders did not have much influence over organizations that followed a specific code.

The primary understanding during that timeframe was that if a leaders created an influential culture in an organization, the followers were likely to lead themselves. Therefore, leaders were only needed during the change period or initiation, and after that, they would be less necessary, since those who followed would operate per the established culture (Allen et al., 2016). This led to more modern forms of leadership.

Yet all of the theories discussed describe leaders as people who are different from the rest. From a historical view of leadership, a leader is an individual who demonstrated specific characteristics unknown in the rest of the population. And for individuals to succeed as leaders, they must have walked closely with another leader in order to learn specific leadership traits and how to apply them (Oc & Bashshur, 2013).

However, as more theories emerged, this view began to

change. Discussions began to center around the idea that effective leadership is not determined by leaders' traits but rather by the way leaders are able to organize their follower.

In turn, this gave birth to modern leadership theories, which focus more on leadership *styles*. Contemporary theorists have instead viewed front-runners as those who can manage followers and make effective decisions concerning challenging, complex, and changing situations. These individuals do not practice ultimate control over those whom they lead, as traditional leaders did, but work together with the followers while providing them guidance (Joseph et al., 2015).

Modern Leadership Theories

Transformational, Charismatic, and Servant Leadership: First of all, transformational leaders have expectations that they view optimistically, trusting that these hopes can provide the most effective solutions. Transformational leaders empower, instigate, and surpass ordinary performance with the aim of reaching high aims (Schedlitzki & Edwards, 2017).

These leaders are known to exhibit their energy and passion for what they presume is efforts toward the best advantage of the business or situation. They are also known to have an idealized influence over their followers. They act as role models for those they lead, and their followers consistently admire them. These leaders routinely display a positive attitude with their team members, expressing pride in their followers. Followers maintain trust in and respect for transformational leaders at high levels because these leaders consistently demonstrate positive moral behaviors (Avey et al. 2012).

Transformational leaders have the capability to inspire and encourage their admirers by continually challenging them to exceed expectations and by motivating them to perform at high standards.

Communication is paramount—it plays an essential role in the sharing of ideas, in producing optimism, and in making people believe that they can move to the next level of achievement. Transformational leaders provide individualized consideration in which they genuinely show their compassion toward the feelings, needs, personal matters, and concerns of their followers.

These leaders communicate with, show respect to, and celebrate individual contributions and accomplishments, because they believe every member is a part of the team and can inspire other team members toward self-advancement (Hoch et al., 2018).

Some of the organizations that have flourished under transformational leadership include IBM, Apple, Microsoft, and Intel.

Apple CEO Steve Jobs initially had a controversial leadership style, yet upon his return to the company in 1997, he had become a leader fully focused and determined. Jobs believed in hiring the best minds, and that is who began hiring for his workforce. He always pushed his employees to do their best, and that later resulted in a company that was unbeatable globally in the technology industry.

Jobs took his staff on an annual retreat during which he would review the goals they wanted to achieve in the upcoming year. Employees strove to have their suggestions placed on the board, and Jobs would omit those he felt were irrational; in the end, only the top three were considered and become the team's focus (Landis, Hill & Harvey, 2014).

Jobs thereby involved employees in the design of the company's goods and services. He was known to be a persuasive and compelling speaker, and his charisma was convincing enough to inspire people internationally to follow him. He created loyalty among his followers, a positive virtue that has stayed with the company even now. The Apple brand boasts the highest number of loyal customers (Landis et al., 2014).

Bill Gates, the creator of Microsoft, is also known for his participative leadership style. He believes that for the company to experience success, employee input must be listened to and valued. Over the years he has been willing to change his business model and leadership style to focus on whatever the company's needs may be.

Gates' approach and participative leadership style facilitated the growth of his organization into one of the wealthiest worldwide. He developed a culture in which employees were autonomous and allowed to make decisions and utilize their skills without dictatorial governance (Oc & Bashshur, 2013).

Many of Gates' employees described him as a leader who helped shape their dreams and encouraged them to aim for the stars. He is believed to demonstrate the servant leadership model, because he focuses on supporting others and making them better. He is known for continually attempting to meet the personal needs, interests, and ambitions of others above his own.

This style of leadership has extended from Gates' company to the world, as he has initiated a humanitarian and philanthropic foundation that continues to leave a footstep on every continent (Oc & Bashshur, 2013).

What Modern Leaders Want

Current leadership theories are not about creating one super leader, but instead are intended to build leaders who inspire others and work alongside their followers to achieve the most efficient results for their organizations.

Leadership is no longer about a dictatorship or about reprimanding followers or commanding them to "do as you're told" or to follow rigid rules, but is instead more democratic. Followers are allowed to express themselves to their leaders, and on many occasions their needs and desires are acknowledged.

Companies start, develop, and attain excellence through efficient leadership, and modern leaders are no longer driven by personal ego or stature, but by their vision for the greatness of their organizations.

Furthermore, modern leaders seek to ensure that their companies work as a unit, and as such they practice a type of collective leadership under which every worker in the organization is a part of the team. Teamwork, ultimately, has become instrumental in the creation of goals, object-tives, and strategic plans that uphold the vision and mission of the company.

Modern styles of leadership are, in fact, creating a healthier world that includes team members and leaders being mindful of each other and inspiring one another to become better employees as well as better people.

THE TREND TOWARD SERVANT LEADERSHIP

Servant leadership is a trend among managers and leaders in today's business world that is becoming progressively more widespread. Although some consider it an ancient philosophy—more than two thousand years old—the principles and methods that comprise this leadership style are regarded by many scholar-practitioners in the modern era as a cutting-edge trend (Guillaume, Honeycutt, & Cleveland, 2013).

The servant leader's primary focus is to serve by meeting the needs of others. Servant leaders in an organization seek to provide support for members of their team or employees (Mazzei, 2018). The writer believes that serving humanity should be the ultimate fulfillment of every person.

The premise is that servant leadership occurs when an organization's leadership and management staff meet the needs of their team members or employees by giving them the support necessary to fulfill their tasks. Hence, the support that leaders give empowers their followers to accomplish the goals and objectives of the organization.

Organizational Leadership

Safferstone (2005) described organizational leadership as the structuring of an organization, the implementation of strategies, and the selection and training of team members or employees. He further indicated that organizational leadership, in a broader sense, includes various philosophies, views, and styles of leadership, and the intellectual aptitudes of leaders, which involve agility, academic accomplishment, and professional insight.

In their empirical study of servant leadership, Parris and Peachey (2013) cited Laub (1999), who produced an assessment that measured the health of an organization's leaders and workforce known as the Organizational Leadership Assessment (OLA).

There are six critical areas of the assessment that are evaluated for those organizations that are mainly led by servant leaders or that are considered "servant-minded."

Those six areas are: (a) Are people valued? (b) Are people developed? (c) Are relationships established and built? (d) Is authenticity displayed? (e) Is leadership provided? and (f) Is leadership shared?

Parris and Peachey (2013) also described servant leadership as leaders who value their staff's interests over their own.

Therefore, a determination can be made that servant leadership and organizational leadership are conjoined. It is through the channel of corporate leadership that servant leadership is executed and displayed, which benefits the organization and the people who make it what it is and what it will become.

Organizational leadership, in its essence, presents a

platform for various styles of leadership to be practiced to achieve company objectives for owners, leaders, stakeholders, and employees alike.

Seminal Theory

A seminal theory is understood to be groundbreaking, an original concept or ideology that has been proven or verified (Udo-Akang, 2012). Robert K. Greenleaf coined the phrase and concept of servant leadership in an essay he published in 1970 titled *The Servant as Leader.* Greenleaf was responsible for amplifying and modernizing servant leader theory (Gandolfi, Stone & Deno, 2017).

The conceptual research of Kim, Kim, and Choi (2014) as well as that of Smith (2005) purported that Greenleaf's theory of the servant leader was birthed out of a story he had read in a novel, *Journey to the East* by Herman Hesse.

Greenleaf described the story as that of a group of men on a mythical journey who were inspired, encouraged, and motivated by their servant, Leo. It was Leo's energy and presence that held the men together. As the journey continued, Leo disappeared, which caused the group to become greatly discouraged, and the journey discontinued.

One of the travelers looked for Leo, and after years of searching, found him. He came to realize that Leo, whom the traveler had once known as a servant, was actually the leader who sponsored the journey. Leo was described as the group's honorable, great leader and guiding spirit.

Greenleaf saw that the honorable, great leader was first a servant, which is what made him great (Kim et al., 2014; Smith, 2005). Greenleaf highlighted how a servant's focus is on helping others, whether a leadership title has been granted or not, and how helping others is a part of the servant's character, which is a passion that never goes away (Smith, 2005).

Ingram (2016) surmised in his conceptual research that servant leadership is the blending of servant and leader. It is not a notion of either/or; rather, it is a concept of both/ and. "In the end, being a servant leader is not something you do but rather something you are" (p. 24).

Evolution

The servant leadership model has continued to evolve over the years. Sendjaya and Sarros held that ancient monarchies regarded their leadership as service to their people and country (Gandolfi et al., 2017). They further noted that servant leadership has historically been viewed as a Christian leadership model; its influence has impacted a plethora of cultures and societies around the globe.

Some forms of servant leadership were also prescribed in the teachings of Confucius, the Zhou Dynasty, and the leadership of the Bedouin-Arab traditional tribal culture. Undeniably, Jesus Christ was the first to introduce in His teachings that the concept of servant leadership should be the endeavor of every man's belief and daily practice. In more recent history, Dr. Martin Luther King, Jr., and Mahatma Gandhi also exhibited servant leadership (Gandolfi et al., 2017).

The meta-analytic research and data analysis of Van Dierendonck (2011) revealed that by the turn of the twenty-first century, scholar-practitioners began to develop characteristics that helped interpret and exemplify key behaviors for servant leaders. The study that was done by these researchers gave rise to the evolution and additional recognition of Greenleaf's original work. Spears, Laub, Russell, Stone, and Patterson were the most widely accepted and influential developers of servant leadership theory.

In 1995, Spears identified ten characteristics that are believed to be necessary elements of servant leadership: (a) listening, (b) empathy, (c) healing, (d) awareness, (e) persuasion, (f) conceiving, (g) foresight, (h) stewardship, (i) development, and (j) edification.

In 2003, Patterson purported that servant leadership is about displaying virtues—doing what is right on the right occasion. There are seven of these virtues: (a) love, (b) humility, (c) altruism, (d) vision, (e) trust, (f) empowerment, and (g) service.

Lastly, Gandolfi et al. (2017) reported that there were six historical instruments produced for the measurement of the servant leadership model in the past forty years. Notwithstanding, from the 1990s to 2011, those that have been developed during that timeframe specifically, postured a context that provided a clearer understanding of how servant leadership has evolved. All of the tools described serve to support and expand the servant leadership theory.

Research, Theory, and Practice

Gandolfi et al. (2017) determined that although Greenleaf introduced and developed servant leadership among organizations and businesses in the 1970s, it wasn't until near the turn of the twenty-first century that this leadership style began to amass any consequential analysis from scholar-practitioners and experts.

Gandolfi et al. (2017) also noted that a critical objective of the research was to prove that servant leadership was "not simply some utopian philosophy that holds no merit in today's organizations" (p. 351), but it can be an extremely fascinating leadership model that is tested, known, and practiced holistically, philosophically, substantially, and—most recently—measurably.

Mazzei's (2018) conceptual research indicated that servant leadership, according to studies, is an effective and productive style of leadership. In 2016, Adam Grant researched servant leadership and established that leaders who practice it are held in higher regard by their employees. Furthermore, by putting others first, servant leaders acquire more understanding about the organizations they lead and therefore direct their operations more effectively (Mazzei, 2018).

Servant leadership is a theory that has gained paradigmatic recognition in both Christian and other religious organizations. However, it has not been as highly regarded among twenty-first century executive leaders (Mazzei, 2018).

In 2013, Savage-Austin and Guillaume published a

phenomenological qualitative study that determined organizational obstacles that have sometimes thwarted servant leadership practices. These include the organization's culture, an apprehension of revolutionizing, and a lack of knowledge regarding the servant leadership model. The study also provided insight into the potential impact these barriers could have on a manager's ability to practice servant leadership in the organization.

The same report indicated further that if a leader were not given the flexibility to utilize this tool, it could negatively impact the work environment, creating a culture in which employees experience a sense of displacement.

Although previous business practices have dictated that the primary goal of an organization is to be profitable, researchers continue to emphasize the necessity for organizations and companies to embrace leadership methods that accentuate a people-centered style of leading and managing; the servant leadership model is one such approach (Savage-Austin & Guillaume, 2013).

Savage-Austin and Guillaume (2013) highlighted that researchers of leadership models have recognized the importance of leaders incorporating the most appropriate and practical methodologies that will allow organizations to achieve desired results. It was also noted that for an organization to thrive in today's market, management must know the leadership principles, styles, and models that are implemented and practiced within the company.

Additionally, the study indicated that the organizational barriers related to servant leadership practices may assist servant leaders in all sectors of business so they will be better equipped to handle the multitude of challenges that companies face today.

To that end, the servant leadership model requires a partnership between the team member and leader. The recipe for a leader's success includes being able to connect with all employees, to affirm their worth and value to the organization, and to empower them for achievement (Savage-Austin & Guillaume, 2013).

Gandolfi et al. (2017) further indicated the effectiveness of practicing servant leadership and its methodologies. This style of leadership is not linear; it is interactive between the manager and team member, which ultimately allows the organization and the employees to achieve its goals and objectives.

Servant leadership has also been proven to be effective regarding employee engagement. This is most relevant to organizational success in that part of a leader's role is to encourage team members to become proponents of the organization. Employees who give their time and talent gladly enhance an organization's value.

Lastly, the practice of servant leadership enhances the moral culture and climate of the organization by serving as a safeguard against managerial corruption and employee dissatisfaction and high turnover rates.

The Ultimate Value of Servant Leadership

Throughout this study, the research has indicated that

organizations and communities cannot thrive or remain relevant if they continue to employ traditional, task-oriented leadership styles. In all the resources reviewed on servant leadership theory, there was a consistent theme: the empowerment and growth of others in ways that value employees, accomplish objectives, and please stakeholders (Kim et al., 2014).

A CASE STUDY: INNOVATION AND TEAMWORK AT DISNEY

The Walt Disney Company has been successful in the entertainment industry for nearly ten decades. The company has worked hard to establish a remarkable global brand, with operations in multiple countries.

One of the ways Disney has done so is to ensure that its organizational structure is aligned to its objectives (Bowonder, Dambal, Kumar, & Shirodkar, 2010). To accomplish this feat, the organization has utilized a multidivisional company structure called the "M-form" instead of the traditional top-down power framework (Beladi & Chakrabarti, 2019). The M-form is comprised of multiple divisions that are semi-autonomous, meaning in part that divisional leaders devise unique structures within their own division. There is a central division from which top management formulates overall business strategy for the company and coordinates the other divisions.

Disney operates the M-form structure—partly because it wanted to use a horizontal organizational design— through its five business sectors: parks and resorts, media networks, studio entertainment, consumer products, and interactive media. The M-form organizational structure was also chosen because it enables the firm to effectively develop departmentalization that generates positive relationships with and among employees (Beladi & Chakrabarti, 2019).

The most valuable asset to any organization is its workforce, and the most effective organizations utilize their workforce in ways that assure them of gaining a competitive advantage. Clearly, Disney understands the impact of its employees.

In addition to utilizing an organizational structure that benefits those employees, the company has also created an organizational approach to job design that ensures greater employee satisfaction. Through job enrichment programs for its employees, Disney's divisions are guaranteed higher productivity (Davoudi, 2013). This approach to job design makes it easier for employees to be more creative and innovative (Pisano, 2015).

Disney has long worked to remain relevant in the competitive entertainment sector and has done so with the help of its satisfied employees (The Walt Disney Company, 2018).

Competition for Selling Happiness

Disney is among the most influential and powerful companies worldwide. With an estimated $36 billion valuation, the firm has been able to operate successfully for nearly ten decades despite an aggressively competitive entertainment sector that requires companies to be innovative and creative so that they can maintain their clientele and continually attract new business, thereby maximizing proceeds (Bowonder et al., 2010; Kalkan et al., 2014).

Disney is an international organization divided into five segments (Cohn, 2013). To effectively ensure that the company continues to generate more revenue, its leaders have developed an organizational design that promotes synergy within its divisions.

Because it is international, Disney is exposed to a variety of challenging external factors, including intense competition from other companies within the same industry. Pisano (2015) argued that developing an innovation strategy is essential to ensuring that Disney gains a competitive advantage over other entertainment companies.

One example has been the constant advancement of new technologies that companies must adopt in order to keep up with their competitors (Cohn, 2013). The advent of social media, for instance, meant that to capture the attention of the changing market, entertainment companies like Disney had no choice but to adapt their marketing strategies.

The idea, then is to meet consumer needs with the help of creativity, innovation, and technology, which in turn allows companies to generate more revenue (Bowonder et al., 2010). Hence, the need to develop an innovation strategy that will ensure that international companies like Disney can effectively penetrate new markets and ultimately have a chance to dominate the market (Pisano, 2015).

To that end, there are three templates for an innovation strategy: creating a new business model, adding value to the company's services and products, and venturing into untapped markets.

Researching Innovation

Because organizations are required to develop a pioneering approach to increase their competitive edge and improve productivity, innovation strategy has been an area of interest for researchers. There is now evidence-based scholarship indicating that organizations stand a better chance of moving forward within a volatile business environment if they innovate strategically (Bowonder et al., 2010).

Without innovation strategies, organizations are bound to lose relevance, because people invariably focus on "the newest thing" and look for those companies that can best satisfy their needs. That makes innovation strategies a critical element for success in the current business environment (Kalkan et al., 2014; Pisano, 2015).

Studies also suggest that innovation can be divided into two categories: market and technology. Further, the research indicates that innovative strategies help organizations improve their products and services, which helps to safeguard profitability (Cohn, 2013). To meet the new metrics for innovation, organizations must plan strategically and use measurement tools to make sure that the strategies will be effective.

For instance, an analysis of Disney suggests that one reason for the company's success is due to the utilization of something as simple as brainstorming as an innovation strategy (Pisano, 2015). Brainstorming enhances creativity as new ideas are brought to light.

Traditionally, scholars have theorized that there are four types of innovation companies can employ. *Incremental innovation* is used within the existing markets by increasing customer value with the help of current technologies (William, 2019). This type of innovation calls for progressive change in smaller steps, and it is the most frequently implemented kind of innovation.

Another type is *disruptive innovation*, whereby organizations use new technology within an existing market; this strategy is intended to maximize profits.

The third strategy is *architectural innovation*, in which companies use an existing technology but employ it in different markets.

Lastly, there is *radical innovation* used by companies to create an entirely new technology as a way of building a new product or service that can be targeted toward a specific audience (Bowonder et al., 2010).

To achieve its current level of success, Disney has continued to leverage its existing business model by employing incremental innovation (Cohn, 2013).

Development of an Innovation Strategy

Organizations must have clearly defined innovation strategies. Good innovation strategies ensure that organizations can meet their overall objectives (Pisano, 2015). For instance, Disney seeks to attain overall company objectives by employing effective communication channels; this can effectively be realized, in part, through the use of technology for virtual meetings (Cohn, 2013).

Disney has also created successful mission and vision statements. The company's long-term goal is to ensure that it can "make people happy," while its driving force is to be among the world's leaders in the entertainment industry (Pisano, 2015). When embracing an innovation tactic, the company has tied its strategies to its objectives, keeping in mind its stated mission and vision.

Establishing a good innovation strategy also requires analysis of customer segments. As developed by Michael Porter, many organizations use Porter's Five Forces Model when examining the intensity of their competition (Ouma & Oloko, 2015).

Using this model allows a company to expend less effort in analyzing its target audience. Using this model, it becomes easier to identify what customers prefer and how competitor companies have been able to meet those needs (William, 2019). Moreover, understanding what customers want invariably enhances innovation strategies; meeting customer needs also provides a more effective avenue for profit maximization (Bowonder et al., 2010).

Bowonder et al. (2010) further argued that concentrating on "value-added" is also an essential facet of developing effective innovation strategies. This includes creating a unique entity that will help to retain current customers and attract new ones (Kalkan et al., 2014).

Adding value is, therefore, vital. By willing to listen to

the suggestions of its creative employees, Disney has been better able to develop innovative strategies that provide a specific value proposition (Davoudi, 2013). In this way, the company has been more likely to secure a competitive advantage, even in new markets.

The Importance of Competitive Innovation

The success of any business is aligned to its competitiveness (Bowonder et al., 2010). The current business environment is intensely competitive, which means that organizations must find ways to remain relevant. Thus, attracting new clientele and retaining old ones is essential to the success of any organization (Kalkan et al., 2014).

With the help of innovation strategy, companies can effectively maintain a competitive advantage, solidify ways they can meet their customers' needs, and ensure revenue generation (Cohn, 2013). Innovation strategy provides an aggressive advantage for maximizing profits.

As innovation strategy allows organizations to venture

into new markets, it allows companies to generate new income streams. Furthermore, making customer satisfaction a goal of such innovation acts as a catalyst toward clients referring other people to the company, who then become new loyal customers (Davoudi, 2013).

Disney's Current Strategy

Disney has continued to have a strong brand presence globally (Trainer, 2019). Applying Porter's Five Forces model has allowed company leaders to effectively analyze external market structures that directly impact operations (Ouma & Oloko, 2015). With Porter's model, it has been easier for the company to identify customer preferences and how its competitors are also trying to meet those needs. Strategies are then aimed at beating competitors, allowing Disney to stay relevant in the market structure (Cohn, 2013).

Disney's innovation strategy is to ensure that each individual and family are entertained regardless of demography.

Live-action and animated films are produced in various languages so that there is brand reach in diverse populations.

Further, Disney uses job enrichment to ensure that its teams design parks and resorts using themes that are acceptable to local residents, allowing for even greater revenue generation (Davoudi, 2013).

Additionally, Disney uses brainstorming teams that are divided into three categories. The "dreamers" safeguard efforts to develop new ideas. The "realists" look for realistic ways to achieve more modern ideas. The "critics" provide analysis of potential challenges of the newest concepts and come up with solutions to obstacles (Davoudi, 2013).

Using this method is important, because it allows employees to come up with original ideas, ways of implementing plans, and possible solutions to challenges that might occur in the implementation process (Ouma & Oloko, 2015). This brainstorming method provides a path for Disney's business divisions to succeed, and for the company's overall achievement of its objectives.

Could Disney Improve Its Strategy?

Overall, globalization of business activities has multiplied exponentially. Thus, Disney has operations in various countries with a diversity of business segments, which gives it a strong brand presence across the world.

The business environment is continually being affected by change, and companies are required to be innovative so that they can effectively create product differentiation to maintain and attract customers (Pisano, 2015). Additionally, the employment of new technology is vital for companies that wish to reach a larger customer base. Disney, for instance, purchased successful entertainment companies, such as ABC and ESPN, because it saw the potential for technological advancement in those markets.

To effectively reach more clients and secure brand loyalty, businesses should work closely with their employees to create a direct link with their customers. Companies can embrace technology, for example, and use it to create direct-to-customer content (Bowonder et al., 2010).

To achieve that end, information technology teams can develop applications that can be installed on customers' smartphones (Ouma & Oloko, 2015). Additionally, media outreach content should be produced in a variety of languages to eliminate language barriers. And streaming services can include Disney-affiliate content, which can enhance brand loyalty.

There have been reports indicating that Disney's employees work under strict supervision. Yet the M-form organizational design has afforded a divisional structure that has enhanced the link between management and employees (Beladi & Chakrabarti, 2019; Davoudi, 2013). As a consequence, during team meetings and brainstorming strategy processes, employees are encouraged to develop new ideas, though during a very specific timeframe.

Davoudi (2013) argued that to ensure that employee creativity is maximized, it is essential they be given the freedom to create new ideas. One way Disney could improve on this tactic is to eliminate time limits on employee idea generation, as the tension created during a time limitation may hinder them from establishing more creative ideas.

Staying Relevant

Organizations are required to develop innovation strategies aimed at enhancing their competitive advantage. Organizations that are not creative and innovative will not maximize their profits, which are needed for any company to stay relevant, specifically in the highly competitive entertainment sector; hence, an organization must create both an organizational structure and an approach to job design that will enhance productivity.

Disney has remained successful for nearly ten decades due to its M-form organizational structure and its job enrichment design. Additionally, company leaders understand the need to ensure customer satisfaction, which is achieved primarily through innovation strategy.

Disney also understands that technology is an essential element in the lives of today's consumers. To that end, the company purchased different entertainment companies on which it can air Disney entertainment content and that of Disney affiliates. It has also worked to maximize product differentiation with its theme parks and resorts, direct streaming, and animated films, which serves to maintain existing customers and attract new ones.

Disney, like many other corporate entities, has developed innovative strategies that ensures it will continue to gain a viable advantage in the marketplace.

A CASE STUDY:
APPLYING SERVANT LEADERSHIP

The Local Neighborhood Community Church (or the LNCC, a pseudonym) was birthed in 1997 in a historic hotel in a low-income housing facility. The author conducted a consultation at this religious organization during the summer of 2018 in a large city on the West Coast.

In 2008, the ministry, which consists of a church and community center, moved to a privately owned building in an underserved section of the same large city. It is currently located in a community known for its high crime rate, drugs, unplanned teenage pregnancies, health challenges, and poverty.

Throughout the life of the church and during the founders' and the pastor's tenure, this ministry has reached out to the community through various programs and other community-based activities and services. The consultant worked directly with the church pastor, George (a pseudonym).

The pastor envisioned creating an LNCC Community Center, whose mission would be to empower young people by strengthening life skills that promote positive values, healthy habits, and education—resulting in real-life power.

The ministry's vision is to empower communities and transform lives through the work of economic and community development. There are five major components of the Community Center that would be designed to teach high-risk inner-city youth the skills they need to become successful in life:

1. ABC Daycare Center (a pseudonym) (for ages three to five years old)

2. Counseling Center (for families experiencing grief, anger, substance abuse)

3. After School Program/Study Lab (for tutoring and

homework assistance for school)

4. Computer Skills Training (for middle school and
    high school students)

5. Parenting/Anger Management Classes (for resi-
    dents within the community)

Prior to coming to this ministry, Pastor George was an experienced entrepreneur, who operated (along with his spouse) a successful women's high fashion clothing business. He was also employed fourteen years as a hospital chaplain.

Pastor George conducted many seminars on grief and bereavement during his tenure at the hospital. When he was younger, he was an accomplished athlete and later served as a coach at two Christian elementary schools. Pastor George holds a Master of Arts degree in Counseling and is a Doctor of Divinity.

The consultant met with Pastor George for the first meeting along with the Phillips Graduate University field placement coordinator. The first topic discussed was the scope of work. The main focus of the work was on coaching Pastor George and about the management of his organization.

To gather information, the consultant prepared and asked the following questions:

1. What's the background of your organization?
   a. How many years has the church operated?
   b. What do you enjoy about your work?
   c. What keeps you interested in the work you do?
2. What changes have you seen in the last five years?
3. Who are the church's key players?
4. What do you believe the problem is?
5. What specifically would you like from this consulting experience?
6. What expectations do you have of this specific consulting experience?
7. Are there any specific modes or protocols for working within this community?

8.   If this presenting problem were solved tomorrow, what would the organization look like?

Major Programs in the Church

As previously stated, LNCC leaders had a vision of developing the five programs detailed above. Based on that vision, the Community Center had recently been renovated. Pastor George believed that by offering these programs, LNCC would serve church and community members by teaching skills that will help them gain employment.

Furthermore, community and church members will also develop skills for handling personal life crises and interpersonal relationships. Since these are complex programs in a complex community, business knowledge and leadership skills would be required to develop them.

ABC Daycare Center: Pastor George was very specific in requesting that the consultant find a way to obtain a government grant to fund a daycare center for the community. This is due in part to Pastor George's love of children and his strong desire to provide affordable childcare for residents who qualify for low-income services.

In addition, Pastor George was aware that having a high-quality preschool program would provide a much-needed service for the children in the community. The day-care center would offer developmentally appropriate activities and instruction that are both purposeful and playful as well as instilling a lifetime love of learning.

Computer Education Skills Lab: Participants in the computer education skills lab would learn technical computer-based skills along with skills in relationship building. The goal of LNCC for this program is to help youth build the skills needed for academic success. The envisioned classes would teach computing models that make technology easy for youth to adopt and create.

Additional purposes for this program were to create a collaborative learning environment that supports youth as they endeavor to succeed in their regular education and to model healthy working relationship skills for youth.

Family Counseling, Basic Life Skills, and Referral Information: To remedy low adult income and low student achievement, LNCC planned to help families attain financial self-sufficiency and stability through the coordinated services of other nonprofits and community-based organizations designed to assist adults.

These organizations include services offering employment support and financial literacy; family management workshops; parenting, ESL and citizenship classes; and food distribution for needy families.

Prevention Health Programs: The church's plans for this program were to offer a prevention health service. Research has indicated that people in poverty suffer from a higher incidence of preventable diseases, including hypertension and diabetes (CDC, 2017). The church would offer nutrition classes designed to provide information about preventive care for people who already have been diagnosed with a disease.

Furthermore, LNCC would offer community-based,

health-oriented classes, including nighttime Zumba classes, senior exercise and dance classes, and annual or semi-annual health fairs that would offer diagnostic testing. These programs would be offered at no cost to the participants and would be provided by LNCC to serve the community.

In addition to understanding the envisioned programs at LNCC, the consultant obtained permission to review the financial condition of the church. At that point, LNCC had been able to meet its financial obligations. Funds were generally raised through the practice of obtaining tithes and offerings from church members.

Donations were also received from previous church members in longstanding relationships with Pastor George. The church had sufficient cash funds to develop its desired programs.

Presenting Issue

The main goal during the initial meeting with Pastor

George was for the consultant to assess the needs of the Community Center. In the process, several issues surfaced. There was, however, no existing plan to analyze the collective needs, prioritize them, or for how the organization should begin to address them.

After several more meetings, the consultant was able to ask enough questions of enough people to clarify the initial steps needed to help LNCC reach its goal of establishing these five programs. The areas that were specifically identified included leadership development, board development, and securing more financial resources through obtaining a grant.

Methodology

The consultant was able to develop a plan in which various models were used to address the concerns that arose from the data gathering and research findings as well as the original concerns that Pastor George discussed in the initial meeting.

The first approach was Appreciative Inquiry (AI). This approach engages individuals, teams, or the entire organization in creating change by reinforcing positive messages and focusing on learning from success (Daft, 2011). Rather than looking at a situation from the viewpoint of what is wrong and who is to blame, AI takes an affirming approach by asking, "What is possible? What do we want to achieve?" (Meyerson, 2001).

By appropriately framing the topic to investigate what is right rather than what is wrong, the team can move away from blame, defensiveness, and denial to create a positive framework and focus on learning for change and success. AI takes a positive, affirming approach and follows the stages of discovery, dream, design, and destiny.

A collaborative approach and process approach were also leveraged by the consultant. The collaborative approach allows a team to explore bold new ideas and embraces innovative approaches to adult learning by using a partnership approach that allows participants to work in pairs and groups.

This exposure-based activity increases the participants' ability to work collaboratively with different individuals and groups. Additionally, the process approach provides a hands-on method to learning that includes an opportunity for the exploration of intrapersonal and interpersonal dynamics to help people within training modules to process information as they learn the material.

Furthermore, to help Pastor George with his immediate problem of understanding organizations, the consultant suggested that he take a class titled "Organization and Administration in the Local Church."

The course was designed to give students a thorough understanding of leadership, church administration, church growth, fundraising, technology, finance and accounting, and church legal issues. Pastor George agreed, and together the consultant and Pastor George met on Tuesday nights to attend class.

The course learning included the application of and

understanding of the fundamental concepts, theories, principles, and practices employed in church and nonprofit administration, formulating a vision and mission statement, formulating a budget with projected income, writing a grant proposal, and understanding the logic model.

The objective was to: a) develop critical thinking skills that will enable one to formulate, frame, and justify ideas in writing and develop an in-depth understanding of church administration process, b) learn the activities inherent in the process and the related challenges and opportunities, and c) gain experience in solving common and difficult problems faced by entrepreneurial pastors, board members, and executive directors in making decisions at all stages of the church administration process.

Students were also given opportunities to experience the challenges faced by entrepreneurial pastors of small, medium, and large churches by participating in interactive, problem-solving sessions with speakers from various stages of church administration.

To achieve these objectives, the course was assignment-centered rather than lecture-centered. A variety of methods were utilized, including problem-solving class exercises, case studies, readings, discussions, individual and group activities, and guest lectures. Course materials and tools included topics such as "Church Growth," "Fundraising," and "Business Management in the Local Church."

The class was taught by the Rev. Williams, who currently serves as the pastor of a large church in a neighboring county (this church started with five members and has grown to more than 3,000). Rev. Williams is also the executive director of a large center for community engagement, where he helps other pastors take on the work of community and economic development.

Before Rev. Williams's call into full-time ministry, he served as the founder and executive director of the economic development arm of a church denomination, which raised more than $400 million in grants, loans, and contracted service initiatives that created more than four thousand jobs. These programs funded more than two hundred small businesses, created more than two hundred new homeowners, and trained more than two thousand home loan candidates.

Rev. Williams was a board member and lecturer at Harvard Divinity School's Summer Leadership Institute for 10 years. He completed his undergraduate studies with a major in religion, has a Master of Science in social entrepreneurship, and received an honorary doctorate in humanities from an international university.

Results

Pastor George was a complicated leader. As previously discussed, one major intervention was recommending a church management class that taught types of leadership, among other things. The consultant attended every class with Pastor George and reviewed the data with him to help the pastor gain the concepts.

Initially, Pastor George was thrilled. Pastor Williams

took a liking to Pastor George and often invited him into his office to share successful principals about how to grow his ministry. As a courtesy, Pastor Williams often invited the consultant to attend these private sessions as well.

Unfortunately, Pastor George was not able to fully utilize the concepts presented by Rev. Williams in meaningful ways. Furthermore, Pastor George would often fall asleep in class and rarely turned in any assignments.

Next, the consultant met with the leadership team. The consultant was given an opportunity to explain her purpose and facilitate a SWOT analysis of the organization with the leaders. Additionally, the leaders were given opportunities to work within their teams to develop goals for the year as well as the steps necessary to complete the actions.

Overall, the leaders appeared open to learning new concepts; the pastor, on the other hand, remained aloof and detached as he preferred to use a laissez-faire style of leadership when working with the teams.

However, within the business office, the consultant

observed Pastor George use a transactional leadership style to keep the organization running smoothly and efficiently.

While transactional leadership can be quite effective because it involves a commitment to "follow the rules," to maintain stability within the organization, it does not necessarily promote change. Yet the consultant observed that change within this organization was much needed, includeing to the style of leadership.

After the consultant discussed various leadership styles with Pastor George, he determined that a laissez-faire style of leadership should be used when working with the leadership team without realizing that given the business needs of a growing church, other leadership styles may be appropriated for certain circumstances.

A laissez-faire leader employs a hands-off approach, allowing employees to get on with tasks as they see fit. This can be effective in creative jobs or workplaces where employees are very experienced. However, for this style of leadership to be at its most effective, it is important that leaders monitor performance and effectively communicate expectations to prevent work standards from slipping. The consultant did not observe Pastor George communicating his expectations or monitoring team leader performance during this consultation.

The consultant suggested the coalitional leadership style to the pastor, which encompasses building a coalition of people who support the leader's goals and can help influence others to implement the leader's decisions and achieve those goals.

Those who practice coalitional leadership are able to observe and understand patterns of interaction and influence in the organization, are skilled at developing relationships with a broad network of people and can adapt their behavior and approach to diverse people and situations. Coalitional leaders have the capacity to develop positive relationships both within and outside the organization, and they spend time learning other's views and building mutually beneficial alliances (Daft, 2011).

Despite all the leadership style discussions and interventions, Pastor George did not change his leadership style and remained a laissez-faire-based leader. He never took ownership of the development of the community outreach programs and was content to "delegate." However, his delegation bordered on abdication.

As the consultation progressed, the consultant recruited a development team to design the daycare program and write a federal grant. Although the consultation can be considered successful because the church received a grant for a daycare center, it was the consultant's hope that the executive board, upon receiving the grant, would hire an executive director skilled in organizational leadership to manage the grant and see that grant requirements are met.

Discussion

There are at least two ways that this consultation could be considered successful. First, Pastor George did receive coaching and was mostly open to hearing new ideas.

Second, the church received its grant. The success of this consultation can also be attributed to several additional factors: the coursework completed at Phillips Graduate University, the application of current scholarship, and the guidance of the field placement coordinator. The field placement coordinator worked with the consultant and with the clients to establish the engagement.

This resulted in a very clear and useful scope of work. Additionally, the field placement coordinator provided guidance throughout the consultation, recommending interventions and sources for reading. The field placement coordinator required the consultant to keep a journal in which she recorded every interaction with the client. This allowed for deeper analysis during the consultation. Finally, the field placement coordinator provided encouragement and support.

There were many courses that contributed to the success of this consultation. The Organizational Teamwork and Conflict Management course provided the necessary skills for working with the teams at the church. The Practice and Profession of Consulting course emphasized the expected professional behavior of consultants. This course focused on coaching. The art of consultation can best be described as an action or approach used to create change. As such, the goal of the consultant is to find ways that result in people or organizations handling themselves differently.

The final area that helped to make this consultation successful has been detailed in the literature review. Daft's (2011) leadership taxonomy helped the consultant determine the styles used by Pastor George, which were servant leadership, directive leadership, and laissez-faire leadership.

Once those were determined, the consultant could choose appropriate and more effective interventions. As a result of this consultation, the consultant has learned that not everyone is qualified to be a leader or serve on a leadership team and that choosing the wrong people, or people who have personal agendas, who do not submit, or who are inflexible and are unable to deal with conflict effectively, can condemn a team to unhealthiness and frustration.

Healthy leadership teams are built on healthy relationships. Anyone who has a history of creating conflict or relational issues should not be put on a leadership team in which healthy relationships with God and one another are the core values of the leadership.

Additionally, the consultant believes her skills in performing active listening, asking powerful questions, designing action plans and goals, and managing progress and accountability have been enhanced. This consultant's desire for a focus in a future career in consulting is to assist religious leaders and nonprofit leaders who struggle with the business aspects of managing a church or program.

The skills necessary to become more effective at doing so have been improved by utilizing tools in the current engagement that will help other organizations move forward. Thus, this field placement has played a significant role in determining how to interact with future clients.

THE AUTHOR'S EXPERIENCE

Numerous people live in psychological pain. My desire is also to help people who continue to bear scars of childhood sexual abuse and desperately struggle with hidden trauma that interferes with both their spiritual growth and relationships with others.

For many, these "symptoms" were born out of emotional denial, and the breeding ground for them was introduced in childhood when learning how to live with other people. When those family systems began to manifest dysfunction, whether it is obvious (overt) or subtle (covert), our childhood mind began to isolate the source of psychological pain in a safe blanket of denial in order to maintain balance (Friel, 2010, p. 22).

This is equivalent to what happens when the physical

body isolates an infection and protects the rest of the body by creating a cyst around it if it is left untreated too long.

These symptoms are also the ways that we allow ourselves to live one kind of life while convincing ourselves that we have a very different kind of life. And while they serve to give the illusion that we are in control, they are in fact clear indicators that what we have really done is to give up healthy control of our lives to something outside of ourselves (Friel, 2010).

Left untreated, these emotional scars can often lead people to drugs and alcohol addictions, which in turn can lead to criminal records and abuse that can trap people in despair and poverty for the rest of their lives.

Helping people to overcome psychological pain is important to me. This is because I grew up in an environment in which I learned early how to distance myself from the pain of verbal, emotional, and sexual abuse. As a result, I suffered with many and varying needs that included feelings of low self-esteem, shame, blame, and rejection.

From the outside my life looked pretty good. I was blessed to be born in a two-parent home, and I was the middle child. My parents were financially well off. My dad was a civil engineer who, after completing his term in the military, graduated in the top 10% of his college class and was already a homeowner when he met and married my mom. My father was a good provider who loved spoiling his children. He even worked two jobs so my mom could stay at home and take care of their growing family.

According to my mom, their problems started shortly after I was born. Mom said she wanted to go out with her friends. My dad had encouraged her to go, and even promised to stay home and watch the children. However, when she returned, she was met by her drunk husband who was sick with jealousy. He said the mere thought of her being out there without him drove him crazy, and he slapped her so hard she went stumbling into the other room. Terrified, she ran into their bedroom and locked the door, only coming out after he was gone.

Abuse of Power and Control in the Home

Violent words and actions are tools abusive partners use to gain and maintain power and control over their partner.

Most abusive relationships do not start out with a black eye. Commonly, they begin just like any other relationship or may seem too good to be true, but slowly, your partner may begin to subtly blame you for things beyond your control or pick at your faults. This may slowly evolve into full blown verbal or physical abuse.

The trauma suffered in an abusive relationship gradually ramps up. It slowly drains you of self-worth and alienates your support system, leaving you feeling trapped and miserable before you even realize the signs. Regardless of whether you suffer from emotional, verbal, or physical abuse, it can be difficult to comprehend that someone you love, and who claims to love you, could victimize you. And sometimes, those partners may not even realize what they're doing is wrong (Littauer & Littauer, 2000).

After two weeks, and many gifts, she agreed to stay if

he promised to never hit her again and attend counseling. Things got better for a while, but inevitably the drinking and jealous rages started again. Weary of my father's explosive temper and jealous rages, my mother decided it was time to move back to her parents' home and file for a divorce.

During the process, she grew depressed and became emotionally detached. As far back as she could remember she had placed others' needs before her own: her demanding mother, an overzealous father, a jealous husband, her children, even God. Still young and very beautiful, my mom decided it was time to go out and meet some new friends. One of her new friends had a son who took a special liking to me and molested me. This was the beginning of my life as a victim of sexual abuse.

Childhood Sexual Abuse

The experience of childhood sexual abuse can have lifelong effects, emotionally and psychologically, as well as cognitively and physically (Frank, 1995). Physical injury may heal, but the emotional and psychological damage resulting from sexual trauma may linger well into adulthood.

Because of the wounds we receive growing up, we come to believe that some part of us, maybe every part of us, is marred. Shame enters in and makes its crippling home deep within our hearts. Shame is that feeling that haunts us, that sense that if someone really knew us, they would shake their heads in disgust and run away. Shame makes us feel—no, believe—that we do not measure up (Eldredge & Eldredge, 2005).

Abuse of Power and Control among Workers

Life changed dramatically when my dad moved away. Money was scarce, and luxuries were limited. My siblings and I wore each other's hand-me-downs as school clothes. Christmas usually consisted of a new outfit to wear to church and a big family dinner. We discovered the meaning of food stamps and how to pick our tennis shoes out of a bin at the local grocery store.

Despite our surroundings, my mom found refuge in her faith, and it changed her outlook on life. Even though times were hard, my mom used to always say, "Reach for the moon and if you miss there is nothing wrong with falling among the stars." She was committed to ensuring that my siblings and I were brought up in church, which became an intricate part of our lives. We knew not to bring home bad grades and not to cause her any embarrassment. She believed in running a strict household, yet built a home of love.

One summer she announced that she had a special treat for us. We were going to summer camp. It was to be held at the Baptist church right down the street from our elementary school. I was nine years old, and this would be my first time attending a summer camp. For a while everything was great. A van picked us up in the morning and dropped us off in the evening. We spent the whole day playing, swimming, eating snacks, and sleeping.

One day I was selected to be a personal assistant to one

of the youth counselors. My job was to help watch the younger children, help prepare the snacks, and get the supplies. With the extra duties came extra snacks and the privilege of hanging out with the older workers while the younger children slept.

When the younger children would lie down for their nap, my counselor would take me upstairs to get more supplies. Once upstairs he placed me on his lap and began to touch me all over telling me how special I was. This became a regular occurrence.

At first, I enjoyed the special attention. He told me not to tell anyone, saying that it was our "little secret." But after a while I started growing uncomfortable. Something just did not seem right. Finally, I told him I did not want to go upstairs with him anymore. He said that meant I could not be his special assistant and I would no longer get special treats.

I said, "I don't care," and walked out, but not before he started saying mean things to me. I started to cry, but I kept walking. That evening I told my mother that I didn't want to go back to summer camp, and she said I didn't have to; however, I never told her why.

"No matter what the degree of abuse the victim always feels guilty. The aggressor puts the blames on the child, who readily accepts it and starts a pattern of lifetime guilt and blame, assuming responsibilities that are not rightfully hers and making apologies for everyone else's mistakes" (Littauer & Littauer, 2000, p. 105).

However, hurt always needs to be acknowledged and addressed. It does not just disappear, no matter how deep it is or how much we try to convince ourselves we're okay despite it. When we fail to process our pain in a healthy way, it becomes ill-processed by default, deepening the damage of the original wound (Roberts, 2018).

Abuse of Power and Control in the Church

At the age of eleven, I sought solace from the church and began to "counsel" with my pastor. My pastor began the session by asking me questions about my life. Slowly I began to share my feelings with him. I felt compassion from him. I even remember thinking, "Wow, he really cares."

Opening even more, I began to share my thoughts about how much I missed my dad and how I didn't fit in at school. I even told him about the youth counselor at the summer camp. As I spoke, I remember him getting up from his big desk and pulling up a chair directly in front of me. Listening intently, he placed one of his hands on my knees. Gently he began to massage the top of my leg as he encouraged me to talk.

I remember thinking how nice his hand felt. As the heat spread through my limbs and his touch grew more intense, I felt my body respond physiologically. For years, I felt a great deal of guilt over this. I did not understand that God had made me a physiological being, equipped with natural, normal responses that would enable me to experience pleasure within the intimate relationship of marriage (Frank, 1995).

For the next few years, I continued to have meetings with my pastor. From the sixth to the eighth grade he found ways to meet with me. Sometimes he would pick me up from my home in the morning before school and drop me off around the corner from my home after school had let out. Other times he would take me home from church, with others, but somehow he always managed to drop me off last.

I began to ditch school a lot and isolated myself from my peers. For a while, I believed this was my lot in life.

Lack of Trust

From infancy a child depends totally on her mother and father to supply all her needs. She must be loved, fed, changed, and nurtured. The infant can do nothing for herself. She trusts her parents completely. As she grows and learns to do some things for herself, that trust relationship also grows until that day when sexual abuse comes into the child's life.

As I explored my childhood experiences and feelings, I could not remember being physically loved, nurtured, and cuddled, which is food and nourishment to any child. I do, however, recall that my mother was "often upset" and used negative words and name calling to express her anger and disappointment. The results of emotional abuse manifested in my life as I demonstrated low self-confidence/poor self-image and became withdrawn and detached, fearful, full of anxiety, and depressed.

Characteristics of Victims

As victims, children often feel some degree of physiological pleasure from incestuous experience (Frank, 1995). Guilt over this can causes them to shut off their pleasure mechanism and ultimately have difficulty experiencing enjoyment in their sexual relationships.

Children can also shut off their feelings or dislocate in response to a traumatic situation. It is as if their mind goes somewhere else and they are disconnected from their body:

Shutting off emotions is a subconscious choice a victim makes to survive because the incestuous incident of abuse was so traumatic, it triggered a myriad of emotions. For the most part, these emotions are never openly expressed but pushed down and suppressed for years. This defense mechanism helped you deal with intense emotional pain, a pain so great that you learned to shut off the emotion associated with the incident. For the victim, this is not a conscious act, but through trial and error it becomes the best way to cope with life's circumstances. (Frank, 1995, p. 23)

Additionally, Hunt (2010) shared how a victimized person can typically exhibit several of these characteristics:

A – Ambivalent   Experiences conflicted emotions about pain and pleasure and gives mixed emotional signals to others.

B – Betrayed	Expects rejection and is unable to trust or have faith in God or others.
U – Unexcitable	Lacks passion for both good and bad, and merely seeks to be free of conflict with others and has a flat response to circumstances without emotional highs or lows.
S – Self-absorbed	Consumed with self-protection and unable to show sensitivity to others.
E – Emotionally Controlled	Disengages from true feelings and becomes blind to the feelings of others.
D – Dependent on Self	Seeks to be in control because of a reluctance to depend on God.

Left with a damaged sense of self-worth, unhealed victims of abuse develop unhealthy beliefs and behaviors.

Because of a past lack of control, some victims have a hidden fear of being controlled in the present. Therefore, they themselves may become over controlling.

Other victims resign themselves to not being in control. Therefore, they may become codependent. Both types of unhealthy fear and responses can produce negative side effects because of the victims' unresolved emotional difficulties (Hunt, 2010).

During this time, my mom met and married my stepfather. The marriage and move took place right before I turned fifteen. I was transferred to a new school and never had another "counseling session" with my pastor again. I spent the better part of the next two years distancing myself from anything that resembled church—or pain. My new stepsister and I had our birth certificates falsified, and I landed my first job inside a snack bar at a local department store.

Often assigned to the register, I quickly learned how to help myself to the money without getting caught. Later, I advanced to stealing clothes, jewelry, and shoes, all in an effort to show my new friends how cool I really was.

It was during this season, I learned how to smoke, ditch school, party, and sleep around. Inwardly, I knew what I was doing was wrong, but I felt so lost that all I wanted to do was run away from the shame and pain that comes from being abused.

Challenges Faced by Survivors of Child Abuse

Victims of abuse often feel shame, anger, and sadness and can even develop post-traumatic stress disorder, a psychological wounding that is oftentimes unrecognized and misunderstood.

The symptoms that we develop as a result of what happened to us run the gamut of psychiatric and stress-related disorders, from substance use disorders and other addictions, to depressions, phobias, anxiety, personality disorders, sexual dysfunc-

tion, intimacy disorders, over activity, eating
disorders, compulsive behavior, and obsessions.
(Friel, 2008, p. 21)

How true this was for me. In my youth, I tried
everything from promiscuity to drugs. As I got older, I
made the decision to use food to cover up my body. I
erroneously believed if I added a few extra pounds men
would find me less attractive and would no longer bother
me. Like a security blanket, I could use my weight to hide
under as long as I wanted, but in the end my plan fell short.
It did not hide me, nor did it help me deal with my emotional baggage.

According to Hunt (2010), "At the heart of a victim's
wounded emotions is the feeling of powerlessness; a feeling
that one is unable to make healthy choices in circumstances
and relationships" (p. 145). Many survivors of emotional/
verbal/sexual abuse have found it most helpful to see a
therapist, specifically one who has special training in work-

ing with people who have been sexually assaulted.

The fact is, sexual abuse is considered a traumatic event in one's life. Trauma is defined as when an individual person is "exposed to actual or threatened death, serious injury, or sexual violence" (American Psychiatric Association, 2013, p. 271). Recovery, on the other hand, is "the process in which people are able to live, work, learn, and participate fully in their communities" (PNFCMH, 2003, p. 38).

Over the years, I have discovered that the only thing more tragic than the things that have happened to us is what we have chosen to do with them. The words I had heard, digested, and believed—negative words, belittling words, untruths spoken in hurt or anger—had taken root and were destroying my life and controlling my behavior.

As a result, for years I drowned in self-hatred and un-forgiveness; yet, until I was ready to face, trace, and replace negative thought patterns to help motivate a different atti-tude and behavior, nothing changed. This is because "time by itself does not and cannot heal those memories that are so painful ten or twenty years later as they were ten or twenty minutes after they were pushed out of consciousness" (Seamands, 1985, p. 34).

Fortunately, as the Rev. Robert Schuller said, I eventually chose to "face, trace, and release" (Frank, 1995) unhealthy emotional attachment, beliefs, and behaviors. Today, while my life is not perfect, I am enjoying the benefits that come from the results of facing, tracing, forgiving, and releasing memories from my past.

An Appropriate Response

Sexual abuse is not only prevalent in society at large but is occurring within the church as well. Over the years, while many have been helped, many continue to bear scars of childhood abuse and desperately struggle with hidden trauma that interferes with spiritual growth and relationships with others (Heitritter & Vought, 2006). According to the Union Rescue Mission (n.d.), men and women trapped in abuse often have significant barriers to overcome before they can return to a productive life. These barriers often include devastating emotional damage, addictions, criminal records, and inadequate job skills or life skills—all conditions that can trap people in homelessness and poverty.

With this understanding, I began to volunteer my time in the church and religious nonprofit organizations, such as the Union Rescue Mission and homeless shelters. Having a need for more knowledge, I met with my pastor and told him about my personal vision of assisting leaders who struggle with the various needs and business aspects that come with managing the church and nonprofit organizations. He introduced me to Phillips and indicated that he had heard an advertisement about the school and that based on what he heard, it could be a good fit for my quest. This was the beginning of my journey to Phillips.

Phillips provided me with professional skills and competencies through supervised field placements that allowed practicum experiences working with individuals and within organizations. The concept of professional skills and competency at Phillips includes the student's appropriate use and application of management and consulting methods. As a doctoral student, I participated in field placements that provided numerous learning opportunities.

These experiences enhanced my ability to provide professional skills and facilitation of focus groups. These experiences have also allowed me to become more proficient in my ability to consult and to offer the professional skills training and management expertise needed for organizational growth.

Hope for the Future

As I progressed through my graduate education, through self-reflection, coursework, and interaction with psychologists and counselors, I determined that I want to work with children and families. This is primarily because growing up I experienced great pain within my family and the church, and because there is a need for trained Christian counselors who have a passion to help hurting people.

According to Wheeler (2000), an effective counselor is one who works with clients to produce a positive outcome, a positive change in the client's perception or experience of themselves, or a reduction in adverse symptoms.

Ultimately, it is only the effect on clients within the working relationship that can determine the competence of the practitioner, but "it is the responsibility of training organizations and counselor trainers to be the gatekeepers of the profession" (Wheeler, 2000, p. 66).

My ultimate aim is to become an officer in a nonprofit organization that provides services to victims of neglect and abuse. With this aim in mind, I have become an ordained minister, a Christian counselor, and a published author. In 2016, I successfully completed my Master's Degree in Psychology with a double specialization in Nonprofit Management and Organizational Leadership. Additionally, I earned a doctoral degree in Christian counseling and have started a nonprofit called Developing Healthy Desires, with the goal of overseeing a counseling center.

I also wrote a book titled *Wounded Hearts Made Whole*. In it I candidly share my life experiences, hoping that others who have faced sexual abuse and shame will gain hope and, ultimately, freedom from their malevolent aftereffects.

AUTHOR BIOGRAPHY

Dr. Shari Scott is a native of Southern California. Her professional career has included many years in administrative, management, and program implementation. She also has an extensive background in fiscal and grant management. She has worked with children, adolescents, adults, and families as a social worker within the California Department of Children and Family Services and currently serves as Director of Community Outreach Programs for Greater New Light Baptist Church in Los Angeles, providing strategic objectives and goals for the organization and overseeing the development and implementation of community services and outreach ministries.

She holds a bachelor's degree in Applied Behavior Science, a Master's Degree in Psychology with a specialization in Nonprofit Management, and a Doctorate in Psychology with an emphasis in Organizational Management and Consulting from Phillips Graduate University, located in Chatsworth, California.

Dr. Scott has worked as a volunteer in a nonprofit office, practicing servant leadership. She has also authored two books in which she candidly shares her life experiences with the hope that others who have encountered emotional, verbal, or sexual abuse will gain insight and, ultimately, freedom from their harmful effects. She is passionate about servant leadership; her business consulting focus is in teaching nonprofit and business leaders and managers this effective and important leadership style.

REFERENCES

Akins, R., Bright, B., Brunson, T., & Wortham, W. (2013).
Effective leadership for sustainable development. *E Journal
of Organizational Learning & Leadership, 11*(1).

Aktas, M., Gelfand, M. J., & Hanges, P. J. (2016). Cultural
tightness–looseness and perceptions of effective leadership.
Journal of Cross-Cultural Psychology, 47(2), 294–309.

Allen, G. P., Moore, W. M., Moser, L. R., Neill, K. K.,
Sambamoorthi, U., & Bell, H. S. (2016). The role of servant
leadership and transformational leadership in academic
pharmacy. *American Journal of Pharmaceutical Education, 80*(7).

American Psychiatric Association. (2013). *Diagnostic and statistical
manual of mental disorders (DSM-5)* (5th ed).

Anheier, H. K. (2014). *Nonprofit organizations: Theory, management,
policy* (2nd ed.). Routledge.

Avey, J. B., Wernsing, T. S., & Palanski, M. E. (2012). Exploring
the process of ethical leadership: The mediating role of
employee voice and psychological ownership. *Journal of
Business Ethics, 107*(1), 21–34.

Bagley, C. E., & Dauchy, C. E. (2013). *The entrepreneur's guide to business law* (4th ed.). Southwestern/Cengage.

Barksdale, S., & Lund, T. (2006). *10 steps to strategic planning.* ASTD Press.

Beladi, H., & Chakrabarti, A. (2019). Multidivisional firms, internal competition, and comparative advantage: Baye et al. Meet Neary. *Journal of International Economics, 116*(2019), 50–57. https://doi- org.proxy1.ncu.edu/10.1016/j.jinteco.2018.10.004

Block, P. (2011). *Flawless consulting: A guide to getting your expertise used* (3rd ed.). Pfeiffer.

Bowonder, B., Dambal, A., Kumar, S., & Shirodkar, A. (2010). Innovation strategies for creating competitive advantage. *Research Technology Management, 53*(3), 19–32. https://doi-org.proxy1.ncu.edu/10.1080/08956308.2010.11657628

Boyes, W. & Melvin, M. (2011). *Economics* (10th ed.). Cengage.

Bradberry, T., & Greaves, J. (2009). *Emotional intelligence 2.0.* TalentSmart.

Brooks, I. (2009). *Organisational behaviour: Individuals, groups and organisations* (4th ed.). Pearson.

Burns, J. (1978). *Leadership.* Harper & Row.

BusinessDictionary.com. (2019). Organizational leadership.
    http://www.businessdictionary.com/definition/organizatio
    nal-leadership.html

Chimaera Consulting Limited. (2001). Stages of group
    development [Web log].
    http://www.chimaeraconsulting.com/tuckman.htm

Cohn, S. (2013, October). A firm-level innovation management
    framework and assessment tool for increasing
    competitiveness. *Technology Innovation Management Review,*
    3(10), 6–15.

Comer, R. (2010). *Abnormal psychology.* Worth.

Daft, R. (2016). *Organization theory and design* (12th ed.). Cengage.

Davoudi, S. M. M. (2013). Impact: Job enrichment in
    organizational citizenship behaviour. *SCMS Journal of Indian*
    Management, 10(2), 106–112.

De Pree, M. (2004). *Leading without power: Finding hope in serving*
    community. Wiley.

Dictionary.Cambridge.org. (2019). Business trend.
    https://dictionary.cambridge.org/us/dictionary/english/bu
    siness-trend

Eldredge, J., & Eldredge, S. (2005). *Captivating: Unveiling the*
    mystery of a woman's soul. Nelson Impact.

Eva, N., Robin, M., Sendjaya, S., Van Dierendonck, D., & Liden, R. C. (2019). Servant leadership: A systematic review and call for future research. *The Leadership Quarterly, 30*(1), 111–132. https://doi-org.proxy1.ncu.edu/10.1016/j.leaqua.2018.07.004

Frank, J. (1995). *A door of hope: Recognizing and resolving the pains of your past*. Thomas Nelson.

Friel, J., & Friel, L. (2008). *Adult children: The secrets of dysfunctional families*. Health Communications, Inc.

Gandolfi, F., Stone, S., & Deno, F. (2017). Servant leadership: An ancient style with 21st century relevance. *Review of International Comparative Management / Revista de Management Comparat International, 18*(4), 350–361.

Gilbert, B. (2016, December 26). Where are the first 10 Apple employees today? https://www.businessinsider.com/the-first-10-apple-employees-2016-12

Glanz, J. (2002). *Finding your leadership style: A guide for educators*. Association for Supervision and Curriculum Development.

Greenleaf, R. K. (2002). *Servant leadership: A journey into the nature of legitimate power and greatness*. Paulist Press.

Greenwood, R., & Miller, D. (2006). Tackling design anew: Getting back to the heart of organizational theory. *Academy of Management Perspectives*, 77–88.

Greiner, L. E. (1998, May–June). Evolution and revolution as organizations grow. *Harvard Business Review, 50*(4), 37–46.

Guidestar. (n.d.) Get IRS data, plus more up-to-date information from nonprofits for free. http://www.guidestar.org/Home.aspx

Guillaume, O., Honeycutt, A., & Cleveland, C. S. (2013). Servant leadership trends impact on 21st Century business. *International Journal of Business and Social Research, 5*(1). https://doi-org.proxy1.ncu.edu/10.18533/ijbsr.v2i5.94

Heitritter, L., & Vought, J. (2006). *Helping victims of sexual abuse: A sensitive biblical guide for counselors, victims, and families.* Bethany House.

Hernez-Broome, G., & Boyce, L. (2011). *Advancing executive coaching: Setting the course for successful leadership coaching.* Wiley.

Hesse, H. (2003). *The journey to the east* (Reprint ed.). Picador.

Hoch, J. E., Bommer, W. H., Dulebohn, J. H., & Wu, D. (2018). Do ethical, authentic, and servant leadership explain variance above and beyond transformational leadership? A meta-analysis. *Journal of Management, 44*(2), 501–529.

Hunt, J. (2010). *How to rise above abuse: Victory for victims of six types of abuse.* Harvest House.

Ingram, Jr., O. (2016). Servant leadership as a leadership model. *Journal of Management Science and Business Intelligence, 1*(1), 21–26.

International Federation of Accountants. (2014). Governance in the public sector: A governing body perspective [White paper]. http://www1.worldbank.org/publicsector/pe/April2003Seminar/Course%20Readings/08.%20Internal%20Control%20and%20Audit/Study_13_Governance.pdf

irs.gov. (n.d.a). Charities and nonprofits. https://www.irs.gov/charities-nonprofits/charitable-organizations

irs.gov. (n.d.b) SOI tax stats for charities and other tax-exempt organizations. https://www.irs.gov/uac/SOI-Tax-Stats-Charities-and-Other-Tax-Exempt-Organizations-Statistics

Johnson, D. H., & Johnson, F. P. (2013). *Joining together: Group theory and group skills* (11th ed). Pearson.

Joseph, D. L., Dhanani, L. Y., Shen, W., McHugh, B. C., & McCord, M. A. (2015). Is a happy leader a good leader? A meta-analytic investigation of leader trait affect and leadership. *The Leadership Quarterly, 26*(4), 557–576.

Kalkan, A., Bozkurt, Ö. Ç., & Arman, M. (2014). The impacts of intellectual capital, innovation and organizational strategy on firm performance. *Procedia - Social and Behavioral Sciences, 150*, 700–707. https://doi-org.proxy1.ncu.edu/10.1016/j.sbspro.2014.09.025

Kim, S. J., Kim, K. S., & Choi, Y. G. (2014). A literature review of servant leadership and criticism of advanced research. *World Academy of Science, Engineering and Technology International Journal of Economics and Management Engineering, 8*(4), 1154–1157.

Kotter, J. P. (1995). Leading change: Why transformation efforts fail. *Harvard Business Review, 73*, 59–67.

Kouzes, J. M. (2017). *The leadership challenge.* Wiley.

Kouzes, J. M., & Posner, B. Z. (1995). *Credibility: How leaders gain and lose it, why people demand it.* Jossey-Bass.

Landis, E. A., Hill, D., & Harvey, M. R. (2014). A synthesis of leadership theories and styles. *Journal of Management Policy and Practice, 15*(2), 97.

Leithwood, K. A. & Riehl, C. (2003). *What we know about successful school leadership.* Laboratory for Student Success, Temple University.

Lencioni, P. (1998). *The five dysfunctions of a team.* Jossey-Bass.

Lewis, A., & Henry, R. (2006). *Robert's rules simplified.* Dover.

Littauer, F., & Littauer, F. (2000). *Freeing your mind from memories that bind.* Here's Life.

Luecke, R. (2003). *Managing change and transition.* Harvard Business School Press.

Lumen Learning. (2011 n.d.). *Boundless management: Organizational structure: structural implications of the life cycle.* https://courses.lumenlearning.com/boundless-management/chapter/factors-to-consider-in-organizational-design/

Mazzei, M. (2015). *Servant leadership.* Salem Press Encyclopedia.

Meyerson, D. (2001, October). Radical change, the quiet way. *Harvard Business Review, 79*(9), 92–100.

Nedelea, A., & Gupta, R. (2015). The dexterity of leadership entrenches the scholastic organizational performance. *The USV Annals of Economics and Public Administration, 15*(2 (22)), 129–133.

Nonprofitally. (n.d.). *How to write your nonprofit bylaws.* https://nonprofitally.com/start-a-nonprofit/nonprofit-bylaws

Oc, B., & Bashshur, M. R. (2013). Followership, leadership and social influence. *The Leadership Quarterly, 24*(6), 919–934.

Ouma, G., & Oloko, M. (2015). The relationship between Porter's generic strategies and competitive advantage. *International Journal of Economics, Commerce and Management, III*(6), 1058–1092.

Parris, D., & Peachey, J. (2013). A systematic literature review of servant leadership theory in organizational contexts. *Journal of Business Ethics, 113*(3), 377–393. https://doi-org.proxy1.ncu.edu/10.1007/s10551-012-1322-6

Patterson, S. R. (2016, April 14). Priority #1: Servant leadership and follower focus [Web log]. Retrieved from https://purposeinleadership.com/tag/stone-russell-Patterson/

Picardi, C. A., & Masick, K. D. (2013). *Research methods: Designing and conducting research with a real-world focus*. Sage.

Pisano, G. P. (2015). You need an innovation strategy: It's the only way to make sound trade-off decisions and choose the right practices. *Harvard Business Review, 93*(6), 44–54.

Poulfelt, F., & Olson, T. (2009). *Management consulting today and tomorrow*. Routledge.

Priest, S., & Gass, M. (2017). *Effective leadership in adventure programming* (3rd ed.). Human Kinetics.

Richards, D. & Engle, S. (1986). After the vision: Suggestions to corporate visionaries and vision champions. In J. D. Adams (Ed.), *Transforming leadership* (pp. 199–214). Miles River Press.

Roberts, T. (2018). *Wholeness: Winning in life from the inside out*. Zondervan.

Safferstone, M. J. (2005). Organizational leadership: Classic works and contemporary perspectives. *CHOICE: Current Reviews for Academic Libraries, 42*(6), 959–975.

Savage-Austin, A. R., & Guillaume, O. D. (2013). Servant leadership: A phenomenological study of practices, experiences, organizational effectiveness and barriers. *International Journal of Business and Social Research, 9*(1), 68. https://doi-org.proxy1.ncu.edu/10.18533/ijbsr.v2i4.154

Schedlitzki, D., & Edwards, G. (2017). *Studying leadership: Traditional and critical approaches.* Sage.

Seamands, D. (1985). *Healing for damaged emotions.* Victor Books.

Shafritz, J. M., & Hyde, A. C. (Eds.). (2011) *Classics of public administration.* Cengage.

Shelton, H. (2014). *The secrets to writing a successful business plan.* Summit Valley Press.

Showry, M., & Manasa, K. V. L. (2014). Self-awareness-key to effective leadership. IUP Journal of Soft Skills, 8(1), 15.

Smith, C. (2005). *Servant leadership: The leadership theory of Robert K. Greenleaf.* https://pdf4pro.com/view/the-leadership-theory-of-robert-k-greenleaf-carol-2058a9.html

Stone, G., Russell, R. F., & Patterson, K. (2004, June 1). Transformational versus servant leadership: a difference in leader focus. *Leadership & Organization Development Journal, 25*(4), 349–361. https://doi.org/10.1108/01437730410538671

Strebel, P. (1996, May/June). Why do employees resist change? *Harvard Business Review, 74*, 86–92.

The Walt Disney Company. (2018, March 14). *The Walt Disney Company announces strategic reorganization.* https://thewaltdisneycompany.com/walt-disney-company-announces-strategic-reorganization/

Trainer, D. (2019). *Disney's strategy is working.* Forbes. https://www.forbes.com/sites/greatspeculations/2019/12/11/disneys-strategy-is-working/

Tuckman, B. (1965). Developmental sequence in small groups. *Psychological Bulletin, 63*, 384–399.

Udo-Akang, D. (2012). Theoretical constructs, concepts, and applications. *American International Journal of Contemporary Research, 2*(9), 89–97.

Union Rescue Mission. (n.d.). *About people experiencing homelessness.* https://urm.org/about/faqs/people-experiencing-homelessness/

United States, President's New Freedom Commission on Mental Health (PNFCMH). (2003). *Achieving the promise: Transforming mental health care in America. (President's New Freedom Commission on Mental Health publication).* https://www.sprc.org/resources-programs/achieving-promise-transforming-mental-health-care-america

Van Dierendonck, D. (2011). Servant leadership: A review and synthesis. *Journal of Management, 37*(4), 1228–1261. https://doi-org.proxy1.ncu.edu/10.1177/0149206310380462

Waclawski, J. & Church, A. H. (Eds.). (2002). *Organization development: A data-driven approach to organizational change.* Jossey-Bass.

Wheeler, D. (2000). *Understanding variation: The key to managing chaos* (2nd rev. ed.). SPC Press.

William, A. (2019). *Disney's generic competitive strategy & intensive growth strategies.* http://panmore.com/disney-generic-competitive-strategy-intensive-growth-strategies

Wong, P. T. P., & Page, D. (2003, October). Servant leadership: An opponent-process model [White paper]. http://www.drpaulwong.com/wp-content/uploads/2013/09/Wong-Servant-Leadership-An-Opponent-Process-Model.pdf

Worth, M. (2014). *Nonprofit management: Principles and practice* (3rd ed.). Sage.

ÁCCENT ON WORDS PRESS

Thank you for reading this publication of Áccent on Words Press. To find out more about how you can also publish a book, contact the editor, Deborah Jackson, at djackson@accentonwords.com.

For more information, visit accentonwords.com.

Áccent on Words Press